MONEY POWER

MONEY POWER

A Force for Freedom or Slavery?

ISAC BOMAN

ARKTOS
LONDON 2016

Published in 2016 by Arktos Media Ltd.

www.arktos.com

Printed in the United Kingdom.

TRANSLATOR	Isac Boman
EDITOR	Martin Locker
PROOFREADERS	Sam Richardson and Daniel Friberg
COVER AND LAYOUT	Tor Westman
ISBN	978-1-910524-99-2 (Softcover)
	978-1-912079-68-1 (Ebook)

Contents

Foreword

RALF ERIKSSON
Associate Professor in Economics

Money Power is very comprehensive in its scope and truly looks beyond prevailing conventions in comparison to traditional monetary theory.

Boman's work is original and critical, refusing to bow to established authorities. The subject matter is in many ways highly topical, for instance regarding financial crises, creation of money such as Local Exchange Trading Systems, and encrypted or 'decentralised' money. The literature is also original and sometimes gives a feeling of reading a detective novel in which the author finds and dusts off, for example, the economic contributions by Nobel Prize in Chemistry winner Frederick Soddy that the guild neglected and overlooked. Even more peculiar is the discovery of the document *Silent Weapons for Quiet Wars* (allegedly found in a copier by a Boeing staff member in 1986), which ought to have a connection with the so-called Harvard Project that viewed money as a form of energy and was led by Vasily Leontiev.

The serious reader cannot avoid the question regarding the central economic assumption — that decentralisation of information (complete or at least more information) is better and this can be applied on the monetary market. The review of activity behind the curtains of the monetary system, chiefly in the United States, seems to point towards a very consciously created, centralised structure in which a few decision makers are seated as the spider in the web. One might be tempted to disregard the idea as conspiracy theory but clear statements from insiders indicate that this is not the case.

Despite the work's bold thrust and the enormous range of the field, Boman manages to keep his feet firmly on the ground. He does not side with any specific monetary system explicitly, even though a fundamental critical attitude towards the dominating fractional reserves could probably be said to permeate the project. This study furthermore points towards the blind spot of current economics, one that can be localised within monetary theory and administration, dealing with how this centrally governed dictatorship can exist and be motivated within an economic science that otherwise cherishes competition and complete information. It is generally believed that there are sound arguments for monopoly in the cases when it is not cherished but within monetary theory such arguments are conspicuous by their absence. Is the monetary market just a lubricant for the real economy, which can be viewed as completely isolated from the real economy? Are the laws of the monetary economy different to those of the real economy and if they are connected, then how? Would it be dangerous to the real economy if the man in the street understood how the monetary system actually operates (through fractional reserves)? Would panic arise if the general public realised the harsh reality and thereby rule out the use of money, in its current form? Everybody understands the basic premise that for money to function there must be confidence and trust in its existence and stable value. Paradoxically, it looks as though this premise rests on a game played out behind the curtains, from which the chairman of the central bank steps out at suitable times with oracle-like statements, mainly regarding changes to the steering interest rate.

The central achievement of *Money Power* is to expose this blind spot and the research frontier is wide. Its base point is democratic, if not revolutionary, in several regards. Firstly, it reveals the hidden realm of the banking sector; secondly, it illuminates possibilities for alternative, 'competing' monetary systems in contrast to the current monolithic monetary culture.

The book has an exceptional language, especially given that the field is pervaded by some of the oldest and most conventional vocabularies that are to be found within the economic sciences. The text flows gently, is easily understood and at times reading the work is a pure pleasure of innovative thinking.

Money Power is a bold and original contribution to a field that is perceived in mainstream texts as being near to self-evident and unproblematic. Instead, Boman shows that it is characterised by contradictory dimensions and points towards interesting areas for further research.

Prologue

Although economists frequently present their work as neutral, objective and based on irrefutable science, sometimes crucial underlying presuppositions, as the Belgian economist Bernard Lietaer puts it, remain unstated and are thereby kept shrouded from view.[1] One such example within the economic field is the question of what money actually is. The word *economics* is derived from the ancient Greek *oikonomia* — combined from *oikos*, meaning house or household, and *nomos*, meaning law. Economics thus denotes the laws of household management or, in more informal terms, how to manage resources. However, the definition of money is not so clear, even for most economists. What is money? A modern saying tells us that time is money. An older adage inspired by the Bible suggests that money is the root of all evil. Yet another perspective, lying in the foreground of this work, is that money is power. One thing we can say for certain is that money is an underlying force in a great deal of activity in modern civilisation. Yet considering the central role of money in the economy and general society, academic research on the topic is narrow. That is why the purpose of this work is not to summarise the current academic discussion on money but rather to broaden it beyond various conventions that constrain the field. The central question of the work — what money power actually is and how it can be designed and operated in different ways — is explored in three chapters, each dealing with diverse

1 Bernard Lietaer and Jacqui Dunne, *Rethinking Money — How New Currencies Turn Scarcity Into Prosperity*, 2013, Berrett-Koehler Publishers, San Francisco, p. 4.

yet interconnected aspects of the issue. The first explores money as a general phenomenon, contemplated in a theoretical and philosophical context. The second chapter highlights the basic dynamics of the current banking and monetary system, while the third seeks to show different aspects of alternative systems. The epilogue is a summarizing discussion, including central conclusions and some thoughts regarding future research on the theme.

1. What is Money?

So you think money is the root of all evil...
Have you ever asked yourselves what is the root of all money?

The character Francisco d'Anconia
in *Atlas Shrugged*, by Ayn Rand[2]

The purpose of this first chapter is to explore what role money plays in the economy and general society by contemplating it from seven theoretical and philosophical perspectives.

1.1 Money and Value

In 1776 Adam Smith, professor of moral philosophy at the University of Edinburgh, laid the foundations of modern economics with his magnum opus, *The Wealth of Nations*. Smith explained his view of money based on a division of value into 'value in use' and 'value in exchange':

> The word VALUE, it is to be observed, has two different meanings, and sometimes expresses the utility of some particular object, and sometimes the power of purchasing other goods that the possession of that object conveys. The one may be called 'value in use' and the other 'value in exchange'.

2   Ayn Rand, *Atlas Shrugged*, Random House, New York, 1957, chapter 2, The Aristocracy of Pull.

The things that have the greatest value in use have frequently little or
no value in exchange; and, on the contrary, those that have the greatest value in exchange have frequently little or no value in use. Nothing
is more useful than water but it will purchase scarce anything; scarce
anything can be had in exchange for it. A diamond, on the contrary,
has scarce any value in use but a very great quantity of other goods may
frequently be had in exchange for it.[3]

These two types of value remain a basic distinction often made in economic value theory. Smith observed that even though it is possible that
a good with value in use can serve as money, its function as a means
of exchange depends on its value in exchange. In other words, money
does not necessarily need to have anything to do with metal coins or
paper notes but can also, as long as it enjoys value in exchange, exist in
the form of animal skins, cigarettes or digital information.

The general functions of money are usually summarised by three
aspects that relate to value, namely to *measure*, *exchange* and *store*
economic value. William Stanley Jevons included a fourth function,
as a common standard to settle debts[4], which might be seen as being
included in the aforementioned three. As will be evident from the
analysis in the third chapter, different economists emphasise these
different functions, for various reasons and to various degrees.

1.2 Money and Distribution

The purpose of exchange, at least between two rational actors, is to
give away something one wants less to get something one wants more.
Money facilitates the meeting of supply and demand of goods and services by bridging the need in barter for so-called double coincidences.

---

3   Adam Smith, *The Wealth of Nations*, 1776, republished in 1904 by Methuen &
     Co, London, book 1, chapter 4, Of the Origin and Use of Money.

4   William Stanley Jevons, *Money and The Mechanism of Exchange*, 1875, D.
     Appleton and Co, New York.

Money makes simple coincidences possible—that is, a seller and a buyer agree to exchange a good or service for money instead of direct exchange with another good or service.

Money is only a tool to distribute scarce goods and services and does not have a function in relation to goods and services that are in general abundance. For example, no one would pay money for air in normal circumstances. An exception is a city plagued by smog, where air gains a monetary value because of its scarcity. Let us suppose there is scarcity of air in Shanghai because of smog and that the air outside the city is clean. An entrepreneur can collect air in pressurised bottles outside the city, transport them into the city and sell them there. In other words, the entrepreneur allocates a resource from a place of abundance to sell it in a place where there is scarcity of that resource. Scarcity and abundance in that case are dependent on space but can also depend on time. Another air-bottle entrepreneur might just fill the bottles at night, when the air quality is better, and then sell it during the morning rush hour. Demand in that case comes from scarcity of a good or service at a certain time.

Historically, the evolution of money can also be analyzed by considering it as a tool used to overcome issues of space and time. One might suppose that at some point in time, small communities bartered with a nearby community when the local resources, goods and services were not sufficient to cover internal needs. Barter between people from different communities could be facilitated by them meeting at certain times of the year, in a certain place. These early marketplaces made double coincidences more probable and thus made barter easier. The first markets to exist independently of specific geographical areas or times of the year emerged when precious metals, primarily gold, were established as a common means of exchange. In other words, the first money was a means to make the exchange of goods and services more independent of time and space.

In this context, one might note that the definition of 'credit' is based in time, as a temporary handover of a sum of money. Through credit, economic value can be transferred from the future to the present in the form of a loan. A company might take a loan from somebody who has an abundance of capital to expand its business in times of scarcity of capital. The loan can be repaid later, when the investment has given sufficient returns.

In nature, the behaviour of storing abundance to use it in situations of scarcity can be observed, for example, when squirrels build up a food reserve during summer to consume in the winter, when there is no food available. To give up goods and services in exchange for money is in that sense a way for man to do what squirrels do when they store nuts. The difference is that instead of nuts, man stores economic value in the form of money — which in time of need can be converted into goods and services on a market. The market is thus a mechanism by which goods and services can be distributed from times and places in which they are abundant to times and places in which they are scarce.

If a good or service goes from being scarce to becoming available in abundance through all spacetime, it loses its market price. An entrepreneur selling imported bottled water can make profits by contaminating the groundwater in a certain area, thus turning water from an abundant good into an artificially scarce resource. A modern example of conscious efforts to promote similar artificial scarcity is the so-called anti-pirate lobby. File-sharing technology has turned recorded music into a generally abundant good and the recording industry has lobbied for anti-piracy legislation to make sure recorded music remains artificially scarce. Spotify, a service offering a great supply of music in an easily available format in exchange for a monthly fee, is an example of how this industry has changed its products as a consequence of the new market conditions it faces following the advent of file-sharing.

1.3 Money and Virtual Wealth

After receiving the Nobel Prize in Chemistry in 1921 for his research on radioactivity, the English chemist Frederick Soddy unexpectedly turned to economics to work out a perspective on the field rooted in the laws of physics. Soddy defined the role of money as a social 'accounting and distributing mechanism' and argued that monetary policy would be better described as 'weights and measures policy' that, like the metric system, should abide by the strict principles of physics.[5] He broke many conventions and as a result of the four works he published between 1921 and 1934 was recorded as an oddball in the history books. Among other things, he advocated five economic reforms consisting of abandoning the gold standard, floating exchange rates of currencies, using public surpluses and deficits for contracyclical financial policy, establishing a statistical bureau to introduce a consumer price index, and removing the privilege of commercial banks to create money through the system based on fractional reserves (see chapters 2.2 and 3.2). The first four reforms are part of current practice and only the fifth goes beyond today's customs. The central take-off point for Soddy's reasoning was ergosophy (from the Greek word *ergo*, meaning work), which, according to his way of using the concept, refers to comprehension of the relation between energy and human existence on an individual and collective level. The ergosophical perspective presupposes that energy consumption in various forms is a basic prerequisite for the creation of economic value. One might note that the concept of 'discharging a debt' fits in well with the ergosophical perspective. Soddy writes:

---

5   Frederick Soddy, *The Role of Money*, 1934, George Routledge and Sons, London, pp. 32, 163.

> Money is a right of action against the community to supply goods and services or, what is the same thing, to discharge the debt incurred [by the community] through obtaining them from the vendor…[6]

He describes his views on the origin of money's value in the following way:

> Its exchange value depends, in fact, simply on the amount of wealth people voluntarily prefer to go without rather than to possess. The value of money depends to be sure on how much people want money but the prevailing loose and confusing phrase as 'people wanting money' makes it necessary to add 'instead of wealth'… The aggregate of exchangeable goods and services that the community continuously and permanently goes without (though *individual* money owners can instantly demand and obtain it from other individuals) the author terms the Virtual Wealth of the community.[7]

The exchange value of money has its origin, according to Soddy, in what he terms virtual wealth, a concept that touches on the time aspect of money discussed above. The time aspect shows why money naturally develops from barter in which the need for double coincidence demands both parties have exactly the good or service the other wants and that they are further prepared to exchange them against each other. Money makes it possible to make indirect exchange — that is, one party has something he is willing to give up for money that the other party is both capable of buying and willing to buy with money. The selling party can then use his money in exchange for another good or service without a need to specify exactly which good or service that might be. Direct exchange means that all goods and services given up in a certain exchange are immediately tied to another good or service. Farmers, for example, who reap what has been sown during a limited period of the year, need to receive the goods and services exchanged for

---

6   Soddy p. 46.

7   Soddy pp. 33, 36.

the crops over the whole year and when need arises — which makes direct exchange impractical. The function of money, according to Soddy, is to bridge the time gaps due to spasmodic production — that is, production distributed unevenly over time.[8] The point can be illustrated with a simplified economy in which grain is the one and only good. In the fall, the government (or the institution issuing money) prints the whole money supply of the economy that is used to buy the crops. The harvest is then put in storage in the government's warehouse. All *virtual* wealth at this point exists in the farmer's hands, while all *real* wealth is in the government's storage facility. Over the year, the farmer can use the money to buy crops as virtual wealth is converted back into real wealth and survival is guaranteed over the whole year. At the time of next year's harvest, the money has returned to the government and the crops have been consumed. The same money can then be used to buy the new year's harvest and thus the flow of virtual wealth and goods proceeds between the actors in the economy.[9] Soddy emphasises that money is not a synonym for virtual wealth but that money should have the same relationship with virtual wealth as food coupons to food, or theatre tickets to a theatre piece. In his last book, 1934's *The Role of Money — What it is and what it should be*, Soddy sums up his central thesis on money with this poetical string:

> Money is the NOTHING
> you get for SOMETHING
> before you can get ANYTHING.[10]

Money has, in general, no value in use in itself but represents a *claim* on goods and services towards the community in which the community has purchasing power.

---

8 Soddy p. 98.

9 Soddy p. 105.

10 Soddy p. 24.

The owner has obtained this deposited claim by giving up some kind of good or service in the past, in exchange for a credit that can be converted into another good or service in the future. According to Soddy, it is easier to understand the real function of money by asking how it is gained, as a 'nothing' one gets for a 'something', rather than how it is used, which is as a 'nothing for anything'.[11] One might further clarify that money is the 'nothing *you have confidence in*', a 'nothing' one trusts can be converted back to a 'something' at a later date.

Soddy makes a point by advocating that a paper bill for this reason should not be marked with the words 'promise to pay' but with 'value received', to emphasise the fact that money comes to an individual as he gives up real economic value in the form of a good or service in exchange for money.[12] By Soddy's reasoning, money in itself is a form of credit against goods or services by which one gives away a good or a service in exchange for a claim on an equivalent good or service in the future.

1.4 Money as Economic Energy

The anonymous author of *Silent Weapons for Quiet Wars*, dated to 1979, stated that it was classified. The document came to light when a Boeing employee found it in a copier in 1986 and with the advent of the internet it was made public. The document's author claims its content has formed a basis for the economic and political policy of the Bilderberg Group since its first meeting at the Hotel de Bilderberg in the Netherlands in 1954. Because of the group's utter lack of transparency, it is difficult to get a first-hand confirmation of the document's authenticity. Yet, considering its sophisticated content, it is hard to dismiss it as the work of an amateur. The main point the work deals with brings

---

11   Soddy p. 189.

12   Soddy p. 172.

to mind Soddy's ergosophical perspective, maintaining that economics should be regarded as a third energy science alongside mechanics and electrics, and that important insights can be made by drawing parallels between the three fields. Inter alia, capacitance in electrics is described as a counterpart to the economic concept of capital. Just as capacitance is a charge of electric energy, it is explained that capital (money) can be viewed as a charge of social energy. These insights were allegedly formulated in connection with the so-called Harvard project, led by the Russian-American economist Vasily Leontiev in the early 1950s. On the one hand, the content points towards obvious aspects of economics which even Adam Smith pointed out much earlier — that money has a function as a medium of exchange for the production of goods and services on a market. On the other hand, the perspective on economics as an energy science has significant implications if it is correct. Among other things, it would mean that the understanding of mechanics and electrics could contribute to a deeper understanding of economics. The prerequisite for maximizing the potential of such an analysis is, according to the author, to make proper translations of the respective equivalents in the three fields. The basis of such an approach is the physical actuality that all energy systems can be described through three basic concepts: potential energy, kinetic energy and energy dissipation.

In *mechanics*, an object placed at the top of a slide has potential energy before it is pushed down the slope. On the way down, the object's potential energy is converted into movement (kinetic energy) and friction/heat (energy dissipation). In *electrics*, potential energy is corresponded by capacitance, while kinetic energy corresponds to inductance (magnetism). Energy dissipation in the electrical sense is the same as resistance. In *economics*, capital corresponds to potential energy, while service production constitutes kinetic energy. The production of goods is the economic equivalent of energy dissipation. In the model presented, capital further includes creation of new money as well as natural resources in the form of energy sources and raw materials. Services are defined as human activity, while goods are divided into two categories: consumables and durables. In the economic-electrical parallel, money corresponds to electricity. A certain amount of currency, such as dollars, equals a certain electrical charge arising from the demand for dollars. Seen from an individual actor, money constitutes a deposited charge that can be converted into goods and services when discharged. For the economy as a whole, money is a continuous current that moves in the opposite direction of goods and services, as a classical model of economics shows:

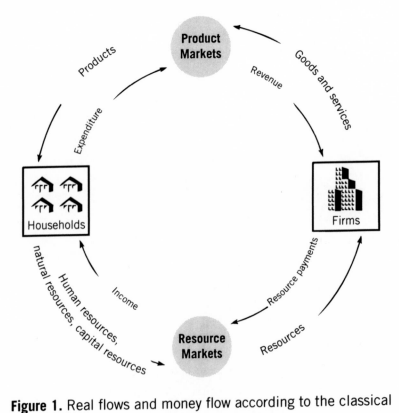

Figure 1. Real flows and money flow according to the classical economic model.

The charge arises both from the demand for money and the demand for goods and services. The current (the currency) moves when economic value moves in the opposite direction — when goods and services are temporally converted into a potential (money) and are later converted back to goods and services in a continuous cycle. On the level of an individual actor, money is thus a sort of economic battery that is charged when the actor in question gives up goods or services. On the level of society, money makes up a potential social energy that continuously flows in the opposite direction of real economic value, stored and tapped according to the decisions of different economic actors.

In this context, it is interesting to note the connections between money, energy and energy flow that are encoded in economic language. Currency derives from current. It is further implicit that purchasing power is an actual power coupled with currency. Bernard Lietaer notes this etymological aspect in his book *Rethinking Money*, written with the journalist Jacqui Dunne, in which he regards the economic system as a circulatory system of energy, information and resources that also finds an equivalent in biological flows.[13]

> All complex flow networks, like the human immune system, natural ecosystems, and biological systems, consist of complex flows of energy, information and resources. Though complex, their behavioural patterns are predictable, independent of what flows through them, be it biomass in an ecosystem, information in a social system, blood in a circulatory system, electrons in an electrical circuit, or money in an economy.

From the observation that biomass is a way in which nature stores the energy of the sun, which is carried on in the food chain, Lietaer then draws a parallel with money and points out the etymologically interesting word *currency*:

---

13 Lietaer and Dunne, p. 61.

Economic systems are similar [to biological systems]: Money flows from one economic agent to another; outputs of one business serve as inputs to other enterprises or to a final consumer in a vast web that processes and circulates energy, information and resources through the entire planet. [...]

Viewing economics as flow systems highlights money's primary function as a medium of exchange. From this perspective, money is to the real economy what biomass is to an ecosystem or what blood is to the human body. [...]

In economies, currency (with its root interestingly in the word *current* or *flow*) circulates among nations, businesses and individuals. Money must continue to move in sufficiency throughout the entire system because poor distribution will strangle the supply side of the economy, the demand side, or both.

Both Soddy's and the earlier mentioned document's descriptions of money chime with Lietaer's perspective on money as corresponding to sun energy stored in biomass flowing down the value chain. Money, from this point of view, is a way for humans to store economic energy that circulates in the economy, something that lets them catalyze processes in the economic system and which generally allows the exchange system to work as a synergetic whole.

1.5 Money as Programming

Processes in different flows can elapse in different ways depending on the different conditions that are in play. It is thus relevant to briefly mention another parallel Lietaer makes, between money and computer software.[14] A program in a general sense is a list of instructions or procedures to be followed. In the context of computer software, a program denotes organised instructions to a computer. Monetary systems and

---

14   Lietaer and Dunne, p. 15.

computer software are similar in that they can be programmed in different ways, with different consequences for the computer as well as for the economy. Viewing money as a digital program is not just a metaphor but rather a direct description of the modern monetary system, which to a great extent exists in digital form and in a very literal sense is programmed. However, in its foundation money is not a digital but a social program — a conscious or unconscious agreement between people based on social customs or legislation. Considering monetary systems as programs is valuable as it makes clear the actuality that the programming of different monetary systems can vary substantially.

1.6 Money as Capital

In financial contexts, money is often referred to as capital. Capital, in turn, is a broader concept that includes more than money. The Swedish-language encyclopedia Nationalencyklopedin describes capital as one of the most ambiguous and disputed concepts in economics.[15] Karl Marx, for example, defined capital as some kind of value that can be used to create more value.[16] The word comes from the Latin *capitális*, 'pertaining to the head', and was originally a term for financial funds that gave returns in the form of interest. Later, it came to be a term for the means of production and assets in general. One way to frame capital as a concept is to consider three different approaches to resource management. Resource management takes place in four stages: resource gathering (allocation), production, distribution and consumption (usage). Looking at the market economy, the command (planned) economy and what one might call the network economy,

---

15 *Nationalencyklopedin*, 'kapital', http://www.ne.se/ as of November 24, 2014.

16 *Encyclopedia of Marxism*, 'capital', http://marxists.org/glossary/terms/c/a. htm#capital as of January 2, 2015.

one might distinguish three forms of capital that drive and regulate
the four stages of resource management in the respective systems.[17] In
the market economy, the management is driven by *financial* capital, or
money in a classical sense. The command economy of the public sector
operates by means of *political* capital through political-bureaucratic
orders that direct how resources are to be gathered and how goods
and services are to be produced and distributed. The willingness to
obey and the ability to execute the orders of the state machinery,
depending on trust in the good intentions of the state and/or fear of
punishment, is what political capital aims at in this context. Financial
capital is based on the principle of positive extrinsic motivation, by
which different types of activity happen in exchange for different types
of rewards in the form of money. Political capital is based on negative
extrinsic motivation, by which resource allocation such as taxation
is ultimately executed under threat of different types of sanction,
including fines and imprisonment. The term command economy is
clearer in this context as it emphasises the basic principle of negative
extrinsic motivation of the public sector better than the term 'planned
economy' does. A third and less noted dimension is the network
economy, which operates by voluntary activity and inner motivation
as a central factor. The network economy executes the four stages of
allocation, production, distribution and consumption by utilizing the
potential in so-called *social* capital, which includes the will and ability
to use time, money or other resources outside of the market and the
state based on voluntary activity. The voluntary sector is an example of
the dynamics of the network economy, in which different goods and
services are produced and distributed outside of market and state. In
the command economy as well as in the network economy, money is
not an absolutely necessary ingredient for these forms of capital to be
converted into production of goods and services. At the same time,

17 Isac Boman, *Nätverksekonomi*, Bachelor's thesis, Åbo Akademi University, 2011.

money *can* make up an ingredient. In democratic nations, such as the author's home country Finland, political capital is generally first transformed into financial capital when the state taxes the citisens and, once taxes have been collected, uses the money to produce public goods and services. To some degree, even Finnish political capital is transformed into goods and services without the market as an intermediary. One such example is compulsory national service. Alongside the negative extrinsic motivation, there is certainly often an aspect of voluntary motivation to defend the fatherland — but ultimately the threat of public sanctions guarantees that the recruits complete their military service in exchange for just a marginal financial compensation. Social capital can also catalyze economic processes without the market as an intermediary by using voluntary contributions in the form of work and resources for a certain cause. Wikipedia is a modern example of how social capital is utilised at a larger scale. In the case of Wikipedia, one might at the same time notice that a part of the social capital is converted into financial capital in the form of monetary donations, which are used to pay a few employees and operating costs.

Financial, political and social capital all have the capacity to catalyze economic processes and together make up a synergetic whole that allocates resources, organises production and distributes goods and services to be consumed and used in an economy.

Against this background one might, in a sense, view political and social capital as a form of money as these, just like money in a traditional sense, make up different forms of economic value that can be converted into production of goods and services. In this book, money is explored only in the sense of financial capital and thus a market-based phenomenon. However, one should nonetheless recognise that these three capital forms work in parallel and affect each other. In a poor economy, where people in general are compelled to work from early morning to late at night to earn enough money, the social capital is affected negatively because there are no extra resources in the form of spare time or money to give to the voluntary sector. Likewise, it is harder for the state to convert its political capital into money in times of economic downturn, which the public cuts and deficits of European countries in recent years demonstrate.

1.7 Money as a Means of Power

In Russia, a new academic field has emerged within the social sciences during the past two decades. The Western world is at present largely unfamiliar with conceptual technology, which can broadly be viewed as a synonym of social management and organisation. In his book *The Phenomenon of Conceptual Power*,[18] Igor Solonko of Saint Petersburg Agrarian University discusses economics from this perspective. From this view, money is one out of many means of power. A pure command economy is viewed as a *structural* way to perform different tasks in the economy by following orders from a central structure. The market economy, on the other hand, is defined as a structureless way to perform the very same tasks. From this perspective, it is contradictory to pit the concepts of market and plan against each other, as the market can be used as a means to realise a plan in the sense of a program of what is to be done. The market, from this perspective, is a structureless way to realise the plan, while the public bureaucracy offers a structural way to do the same. Let us assume that a totalitarian tyrant aims to build a palace. The tyrant orders a thousand people to give up their resources, including their work, to build the palace, or else they are to be shot. This example is political capital (political power) or structural management used and applied in its most cartooned form. Another leader might build the same palace by using financial capital to buy

---

18 Igor Solonko, *Fenomen Kontseptualnoj Vlasti: Sotsialno-Filosofskij Analiz* (Феномен Концептуальной Власти: Социально-Философский Анализ), Solo, Saint Petersburg, 2010.

resources and workers' services for the same end. Money is thereby not only a means of exchange, it is a means of power which, like direct orders, can be used to achieve a certain result that the owner of the money defines. The perspective on money as a means of power illustrates that the banking and monetary system in itself can and should be regarded as a subject of power with the potential to exert influence on individuals and societies as power objects. This perspective is perhaps best summarised in a quote that has been attributed to Mayer Amschel Rothschild: 'Give me control over a nation's money and I care not who makes its laws.'[19] Even if it is highly unclear whether Rothschild really uttered these words, it is easy to understand why they have been associated with the founder of the storied banking dynasty if one contemplates the modern monetary system and its history, especially in America, which is the theme of chapter 2.

---

19 There are no primary sources confirming that Mayer Amschel Rothschild formulated these words. The earliest source to the author's knowledge is Gertrude M. Coogan's *Money Creators — Who Creates Money, Who Should Create It* from 1935. It is probable that the quote has its roots in a popular view of corruption within the big banking dynasties and that Rothschild has been picked as a symbol of this view.

2. The Modern Monetary System

The people must be helped to think naturally about money. They must be told what it is and what makes it money, and what are the possible tricks of the present system which put nations and peoples under control of the few.

HENRY FORD[20]

This chapter is a summary of the current state of banking and monetary theory within economic science and the general dynamics and influence of the modern banking and monetary system on the body of society.

2.1 Banks and Money: A Neglected Area of Economics

This first subchapter breaks conventions of academic style by enclosing a longer excerpt from the documentary *The Economic Science*, which was produced for Swedish popular science show *Vetenskapens Värld* (*The World of Science*) and screened by the nation's public service broadcaster SVT on November 19, 2012.[21] There are three reasons for

---

20 Henry Ford, *My Life and Work*, 1922, Doubleday, Page & Company, p. 179.

21 *Den ekonomiska vetenskapen* — documentary produced by *Vetenskapens Värld* (Swedish Public Service), broadcast on November 19, 2012. Available on youtube. com as of May 31, 2016: 'Economic Science and the Debt Crisis (*Vetenskapens Värld* 19-11-2012), English subtitles'.

this. Firstly, it is unusual for popular science shows to illustrate the remarkable way in which money and banks have been neglected in economic science. Secondly, this excerpt shows that there are, in spite of this general neglect, notable economists who emphasise how pressing it is to research the field in a more comprehensive way. Finally, the excerpt serves as a suitable introduction to the other subchapters.

JENS ERGON, voice-over:

> How is money really created? It might seem an odd question but as a matter of fact it divides different economists and is a question that leads to the very heart of the debt crisis. [...] Back in time, money was made from precious metals. They were worth their weight in gold. Then the notes came. The banks, ultimately the central banks, guaranteed the value of money. Today, most money is numbers in computers. Cash makes up less than a tenth of all money. Money is not primarily created by a money press.

DIRK BEZEMER, economist at University of Groningen

> When the bank extends a loan, it creates money. Let's say that I want to buy a very expensive watch for €100,000 and I don't have the money. I can go to the bank and ask for a consumption loan. If it's a good bank they say no. But if they grant it, they don't give me a bag of money, they will just take my credit card, my passport perhaps and there will be some things done on the computer keyboard and some signatures, that's it. [...] Now at this point money has been created. This money didn't exist the same morning before I decided to buy the watch and take out the loan. It's new money, fresh money, that's how banks create money. Banks bring new money into the economy as they make up loans. Therefore, if you expend the stock of money, you also expend the stock of debt.

ROBERT LUCAS, winner of the Nobel Prize in Economics, 1995:

> The high level of debt is not something you want to look at. It's not like the country as a whole is in debt. For every debtor there is a lender, so in some sense they cancel each other out.

DIRK BEZEMER:

> This is very strange. Economists often say that debt and credit don't really matter because it cancels out, but it may be a very harmful situation if, let's say, half of the households have to leave their house because they can't service their debts, or they pay so much in mortgage service every month so that effective demand is low.

> [...]

STEVE KEEN, economist at University of Western Sydney:

> The reason most economists didn't see it, is that they built models of the macro-economy that exclude banks, money and debt. I know it sounds outrageously stupid to anybody who isn't an economist. The ironic thing is that they are right. It is outrageously stupid. [...] It's insane to have a model of the macro economy that excludes bank, money and debt. You don't even know if they are misbehaving, that's irrelevant, off to the side. That's why the vast majority of economists had no idea [that the financial crisis of 2008] was coming.

JENS ERGON:

> It sounds almost too mind-boggling to be true. But this picture is confirmed by several scientists.

MICHAEL KUMHOF, economist at the International Monetary Fund:

> To a layman, it sounds like a joke. What is he talking about? He can't be serious. That macro-economists have been thinking about the macro-economy without banks. But that is exactly what has been happening over the last 30 years. Anything regarding banks was fringe activity. [...]

> The way macro-economists have traditionally thought about banks is as intermediaries. Basically the banks sit there, they wait for deposits to arrive and if they have enough deposits they lend them out to somebody else. And that is completely wrong. It's a wrong model of banks, because what happens in reality is exactly the opposite. I'm a banker, so I know

that's how it works and you can read on many central bank websites that it's how it works. When the banks decide that the economy is good and are optimistic, they don't need to wait for any deposits because when they make a loan they create the deposit. Banks create money out of thin air.

[...]

ROBERT LUCAS:

I think it's nonsense [that flawed theories were behind the crisis]. It's just crazy to get rid of neoclassical economics, at least we have got to have something else on the table.

MICHAEL KUMHOF:

People have built their entire careers on this for 20, 30, 40 years. These people are Nobel Prize winners and very important people. I don't expect that people like that are going to give that view up from one day to the next.

[...]

DIRK BEZEMER:

There is a very widespread feeling that economics has missed out on something important. One answer is that we missed out on the role of credit and debt in the economy. Others say that the new paradigm needs to be based on complexity.

Rescue packages, banking unions and debt crises are terms that are intimately linked to the monetary systems and often used in economic journalism. At the same time, concepts like these are rarely explained in a context deep and broad enough for a reader to grasp their actual meaning. However, Harvard professor John Kenneth Galbraith argued that the process by which money is created is not necessarily difficult to understand:

The study of money, above all other fields in economics, is the one in which complexity is used to disguise truth or evade truth, not to reveal it. [...]

The process by which banks create money is so simple that the mind is repelled. Where something so important is involved, a deeper mystery seems only decent.[22]

Murray Rothboard, an economist of the Austrian School, draws a parallel between the monetary system and the character of the Wizard of Oz, who in Frank Baum's tale of the same name built his power on an illusion until he was exposed:

Money and banking have been made to appear as mysterious and arcane processes that must be guided and operated by a technocratic elite. They are nothing of the sort. In money, even more than the rest of our affairs, a malignant Wizard of Oz has tricked us.[23]

A straightforward way to explore the current basis of the monetary system is to go back to the era of *The Wizard of Oz*, which was published in the U.S. in 1900. At the beginning of the 20th century, the activities of the Rockefeller family were even catching the eye of the average Joe and there was a growing concern over what long-term consequences the domination on the American market by the Rockefellers and other heavy actors would have. In February 1913, the Pujo Committee, appointed by Congress and named after congressman Arséne Pujo, even presented detailed documentation showing that the Rockefellers together with a small group of financial leaders had gained extensive

22 John Kenneth Galbraith, *Money: Whence it came, where it went,* 1975, repub-lished in 2001, Houghton Mifflin Books, Boston, pp. 5, 18.

23 Murray Rothboard, *Making Economic Sense* (Second edition published 2005, first edition 1995), Ludwig van Mises Institute, p. 294.

control over America's industry and financial market.[24] William Rockefeller (co-founder of Standard Oil), J. P. Morgan and Paul Warburg are mentioned in the report as central players in this group. The Pujo report contributed to increasing calls from the public to reform banking and monetary legislation, a scenario that the financial magnates in question were already well prepared for. As early as November 1910, representatives of the banking dynasties Rockefeller, Morgan, Warburg and Rothschild had, under great secrecy, met on Jekyll Island on America's East Coast to sketch out their own legislation proposals — which would benefit their interests at the expense of competitors and the general public. The attendees denied for a long time that such a meeting had taken place and those who claimed conspiracy were ignored or ridiculed by mainstream media and science. Paul Warburg later confirmed his participation in the meeting, as well as the precautions of secrecy, in his book *The Federal Reserve System: Its Origin and Growth*, published in 1930:

> In November 1910, I was invited to join a small group of men who, at Senator Aldrich's request, were to take part in several days' conference with him, to discuss the form that the new banking bill should take.
>
> [...] The results of the conference were entirely confidential. Even the fact that there had been a meeting was not permitted to become public.[25]

Just over 100 years later, this meeting is confirmed openly, as well as its central importance in creating the Federal Reserve System (FRS). One example of this is the jubilee conference *A Return to Jekyll Island — The*

---

24 *Report of the Committee Appointed Pursuant to House Resolutions 429 and 504, 1912–1913* — Pujo Committee Report, available on http://www.scribd.com/doc/34121180/Pujo-Committee-Report-Report-of-the-Committee-Appointed-Pursuant-to-House-Resolutions-429-and-504-1912-1913-Pujo-Committee-Report, as of May 31, 2016.

25 Paul Warburg, *The Federal Reserve System: Its Origin and Growth*, 1930, New York, Macmillan, vol. 1 pp. 58, 60.

Origins, History and Future of the Federal Reserve, held in 2010 on Jekyll Island with the chairman of the Federal Reserve, Ben Bernanke, and his predecessor Alan Greenspan among the attendees.[26] The American historian G. Edward Griffin's best-known work *The Creature From Jekyll Island* (1994) is a detailed documentation of the whole dramatic course of events which preceded and succeeded the implementation of the Federal Reserve Act, the new banking bill passed in Congress on December 23, 1913.[27] There are many indicators that this act was the very proposal developed on Jekyll Island in 1910 to serve the interests of the big banking houses. A summary of its design follows in the next subchapter.

2.2 Summary of the Current Banking and Monetary System

Mike Maloney's educational video *The Hidden Secrets of Money* is a summary of the dynamics of the American system and, currently, also of most other banking and monetary systems which in most cases are very similar to the FRS.[28]

A handbook published in 1961 by the Federal Reserve of Chicago Public Information Center called *Modern Money Mechanics*[29] also describes the most essential aspects of these dynamics. The modern

---

26 Michael D. Bordo and William Roberds, *A Return to Jekyll Island — The Origins, History and Future of the Federal Reserve,* 2013, Cambridge University Press, Cambridge.

27 G. Edward Griffin, *The Creature from Jekyll Island,* first edition published 1994, American Media, California.

28 Mike Maloney, *Hidden Secrets of Money,* Part 4, http://hiddensecretsofmoney. com/videos/episode-4 as of May 31, 2016.

29 Federal Reserve Bank of Chicago Public Information Center, *Modern Money Mechanics — A Workbook on Bank Reserves and Deposit Expansion,* first published in 1961, available online in an updated version from 1994.

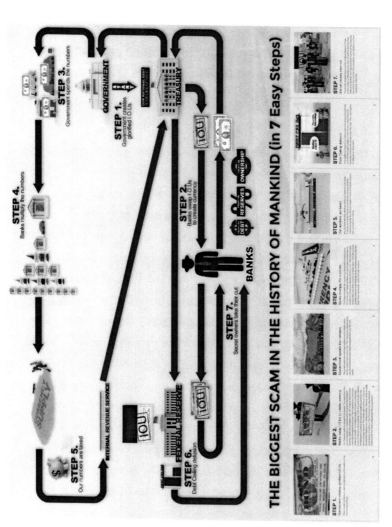

Figure 2. Flowchart of the modern banking and monetary system from the video 'Hidden Secretsof Money'. (Full resolution: www.hiddensecretsofmoney.com/blog/Ambassador-Kit)

banking and monetary system can be summarised in seven points illustrated on figure 2 with FRS as an example:

1) Issuance of bonds

A government can get money by lending them on the market. In practice, the government does this by issuing bonds, that is to say IOUs sold on the open market to banks and other financial institutions. When the government does this it thereby raises the public debt.

2) Bonds get converted into currency

Government bonds make up the base for how money is created in the next phase, when bonds are converted into currency. The bank or the institution that has bought the bond can choose to sell the bond to the central bank. The central bank can, depending on its current policy, also be open to buying types of bonds other than government bonds, such as corporate bonds. The central bank — regardless of whether it is the Federal Reserve, the European Central Bank or the Swedish National Bank — finances these purchases by using the bank note press, or the credit press which represents bank notes in the form of digital central bank money. This is the way cash is created, in the case of the U.S. so-called Federal Reserve notes. By purchasing and selling bonds, the central bank influences the money supply and thereby also the general interest level. Purchase of bonds expands the money supply, which has a repressing effect on interest levels. The opposite applies if the central bank sells bonds and the money supply consequently shrinks. Wright Patman, chairman of Congress' House Banking and Currency Committee in the 60s, explained how the process of central bank money creation works in practice:

> When the Federal Reserve writes a check for a government bond it does exactly what any bank does, it creates money. [...]

And if the recipient of the check wants cash, then the Federal
Reserve can oblige him by printing the cash — Federal Reserve
notes — which the check receiver's commercial bank can then
hand over to him.[30]

On an international level, the International Monetary Fund (IMF)
can create money by granting Special Drawing Rights (SDRs),
which give a right to redeem central bank money in any of the
IMF's member central banks.

3) Financing the budget of the government

The money the government gets from selling bonds is then used
to finance eventual deficits in the public sector. When money is
consequently put into circulation it is multiplied by the banking
system in the next step, the multiplier effect.

4) The multiplier effect

The multiplier effect in this sense is not to be mixed up with Keyne's
multiplier effect, which describes how an expanded money supply
has positive effects on the overall economy during times of low
economic activity. The multiplier effect in this model refers to how
public employees, or other actors paid for by public purchasing,
put their money in a bank and how the system based on fractional
reserves then multiplies the amount of money put into the banking system — tenfold or more. Under this process, more than 90
per cent of the money supply is issued as loans by commercial
banks. Part of the explanation as to why housing prices tend to be
disproportionately high is that a significant share of this money is
channelled into the economy in the form of mortgages. A separate
bank can carry out the multiplicator without interaction with other
banks. The Chicago Fed handbook explains:

---

30 Wright Patman, *A Primer on Money*, 1964, Government Printing Office,
Washington, p. 34.

[Banks] do not really pay out loans from the money they receive as deposits. If they did this, no additional money would be created. What they do when they make loans is to accept promissory notes in exchange for credits to the borrowers' transaction accounts. [...]

[Banks] can build up deposits by increasing loans and investments so long as they keep enough currency on hand to redeem whatever amounts the holders of deposits want to convert into currency. This unique attribute of the banking business was discovered many centuries ago. It started with goldsmiths.[31]

Historically, a bank could grant new credit for loans or for its own investments in the form of bank notes, as long as the notes were trusted to be redeemable in gold when demanded. Today, banks no longer need to have gold available, just a sufficient amount of cash to meet the demands of depositors when they ask for it. The promise of the modern bank is to have the money available when you want it, not to store it. It is also possible for a bank to create credit to use for investment. Many countries do not have any requirements on how much cash needs to be available. What determines the amount of credit a bank can create is the so-called capital requirement. Olof Sandstedt on The Swedish National Bank writes:

In Sweden, just as in many other countries, there isn't any cash requirement. Instead the lending of banks is ultimately regulated by a capital requirement. The capital requirement is defined in the so-called Basel rules and somewhat simplified means that the banks must keep a certain amount of equity capital (share capital and retained earnings) in relation to their lending (eight per cent of the risk-adjusted lending). In detail, the capital requirement differs somewhat from the cash requirement, but the

---

31 See note 29, pp. 6, 3.

mechanism is basically the same [as fractional reserves based on cash requirement].[32]

5) The role of the citizens

If the banking system is threatened by collapse because of the system based on fractional reserves, it is primarily the state that, through tax money, guarantees to maintain stability by granting rescue packages to failing banks. As a result of the Single Resolution Mechanism, part of the so-called Banking Union, it has even been made judicial praxis in Europe that members of the European Monetary Union collectively fund such rescue packages for financial institutions at risk of breakdown. Besides similar welfare packages, the state pays interest on government bonds — that is, on its public debt. As the money in circulation is based on such bonds, in practical terms it means the citizens pay tax in order to even *have* a monetary system.

An American report published by the Grace Commission, supervised by the government of Ronald Reagan, came to the conclusion that 'all individual income tax revenues are gone before one nickel is spent on the services which taxpayers expect from their government'. This is because the size of the federal income tax revenue is equalled by that of the costs of the federal debt and the administration costs of the tax.[33] In comparison, the numbers in Finland are not as extreme as in the United States, which can be explained by the higher income tax and the lower level of public debt in relation to the gross domestic product — about 50 per cent

---

32 Letter from Riksbanken to Henning Witte, http://files.meetup.com/189080/riksbanken%20svar%20pdf%208.7.10.pdf as of May 31, 2016.

33 Grace Commission, *The President's Private Sector Survey on Cost Control*, January 12th 1984, The Library of Congress, Congressional Research Service, US. Government Printing Office, p. 12, http://digital.library.unt.edu/ark:/67531/metacrs9044/m1/1/high_res_d/IP0281G.pdf as of May 31, 2016.

in comparison to 70 per cent for America[34]. In 2013, the calculated income to the Finnish state from income and capital taxation was €8.6 billion. Some €1.86 billion was reserved in the state's budget for interest payments on its debt, which amounted to €89 billion.[35]

6) The debt spiral

As all money except coins are created as interest-bearing debt, new loans must continuously be granted if the interest is to be paid back. If the aggregate private and public debt does not increase and only remains constant or decreases, the result will be economic decline when the money in circulation consequently decreases. A symptom of this dynamic in the U.S. is that the public debt ceiling is continuously raised. As far back as 1934, Robert H. Hemphill, Credit Manager of the Federal Reserve Bank of Atlanta, described the situation accordingly:

> Someone has to borrow every dollar we have in circulation, cash or credit. If the Banks create ample synthetic money we are prosperous; if not, we starve. We are absolutely without a permanent money system. When one gets a complete grasp of the picture, the tragic absurdity of our hopeless position is almost incredible, but there it is. It is the most important subject intelligent persons can investigate and reflect upon.[36]

Hypothetically, if all debts, private and public, were to be paid back, the whole money supply would be extinguished. However,

---

34 Government office of Finland, structure of the national debt, http://www. treasuryfinland.fi/sv-FI/Statistik/Statsskuld/Statsskuldens_struktur as of May 31, 2016.

35 Finnish government budget for 2013, http://www.edilex.fi/data/sdliite/liite/6165. pdf as of May 31, 2016.

36 Robert H. Hemphill is quoted in the foreword of *100 % Money* by professor Irving Fisher at Yale University, first published in 1935, republished in 1996 by Pickering and Chatto, London.

this is not even theoretically possible as there is not enough money to repay the interest, beside the principal.

7) Dividend

The Federal Reserve Bank of New York, the largest of the 12 reserve banks of the Federal Reserve, lists Goldman Sachs, Deutsche Bank and Empire State Bank among its members.[37] On the Federal Reserve website, it is explained that the system is owned by its member banks, albeit not in a traditional sense as it is compulsory for the member banks to own the shares, which cannot be bought or sold. Furthermore, the yearly dividend is enshrined in law.[38] In 1982, it was even ruled by a federal court that the Federal Reserve should be regarded as a de facto private corporation.[39] The money remaining after payment of dividends and funding of the Federal Reserve's operation is handed over to the Department of the Treasury.

As a European example, The Bank of Finland also shares part of its profit with the Finnish state, the European Central Bank and what is termed a reserve fund.[40] The dividend from Bank of Finland to the state in 2013 amounted to €180 million.[41] It is difficult to determine whether central banks other than the Federal Reserve are privately owned. It is clear that its national member banks own the

---

37 New Work Federal Reserve, Second District Member Banks, http://www.newyorkfed.org/banks.html as of May 31, 2016.

38 Homepage of the Federal Reserve — FAQhttp://www.federalreserve.gov/faqs/about_14986.htm as of May 31, 2016.

39 Lewis v. United States, 680 F.2d 1239 (1982), https://law.resource.org/pub/us/case/reporter/F2/680/680.F2d.1239.80-5905.html as of May 31, 2016.

40 Law on Bank of Finland, Finlex, http://www.finlex.fi/sv/laki/ajantasa/1998/19980214 as of May 31, 2016.

41 Press release from Bank of Finland, March 24, 2014, http://www.suomenpankki.fi/sv/suomen_pankki/ajankohtaista/tiedotteet/pages/tiedote11_2014.aspx as of May 31, 2016.

European Central Bank but that does not say anything about who
might in turn own the member banks. In legal terms, the Bank of
Finland is a legal public institution with an assembly appointed by
the parliament of Finland. On the other hand, one might note that
the Federal Reserve has a similar legal public design with a chairman appointed by the president, so this in itself does not make
up evidence for public ownership. On Bloomberg's company index
on businessweek.com, for example, the national banks of Finland,
Sweden, Norway and Denmark are, just like the Federal Reserve,
listed not as public but as private corporations.[42] In the fourth and
sixth paragraph, one can further read that the Bank of Finland is
independent of the state and that it takes orders from nowhere
other than the European Central Bank, and that public funding
is prohibited and public authorities are to be treated just as any
other actor in relation to the central bank. However, it seems to
be the case that commercial banks in Finland, according to current legislation, are not shareowners of the Bank of Finland (and
thus not of the ECB either) or entitled to direct dividends from the
profits of the central bank such as the member banks of the Federal
Reserve get.

Irrespective of whether a central bank in the current system
is owned privately or by the state, the banking and monetary system in both Finnish-European and American context is a hybrid
between a private and a public legal system, in which commercial
banks create the main body of the money supply, while the state
in both cases gets a share of the profit the central bank generates.
In that context, it is really a marginal question as to whether the
central bank in such a system is private or public.

---

42 Bloomberg Company Index at *Bloomberg Businessweek*, 'Company Lookup',
    keywords 'Bank of Finland' etc., http://investing.businessweek.com/research/
    common/symbollookup/symbollookup.asp? lookuptype=private&region=all&t
    extIn=Bank%20of%20FInland as of January 11, 2015.

The historical roots of the current system's basic principles, which are based on fractional reserve banking, can be traced back a long way. The Chicago Fed brochure links them to the medieval goldsmiths, while others track their origins to ancient Babylonia.[43] It is clear that, at one time or another, gold vault owners made the observation that people preferred to keep their gold secure and trade with paper evidence of their gold holdings, and that just a fraction of the gold savers needed their gold at a certain time. Thus one could print more bank notes than there was gold in the vault. Some vault owners did exactly this and lent these notes out as interest-bearing debts in exchange for collateral. Booms developed when the granting of credit was plentiful and the economy was flooded with banknotes. In these times, banks increased their interest income in the form of gold influx. In times of depression, the banks still had a potential to make profit by recalling the collateral of borrowers who could not repay their loans, thus either taking over ownership or selling the collateral on the market. This type of banking is in its nature pro-cyclical: when optimism is high, a lot of loans are granted and they fuel the boom as the money supply increases; when pessimism increases, fewer loans are granted, which consequently deepens the depression. Bank collapses were prevented and avoided by collaboration between these early bankers, who lent gold to colleagues who were hit by a temporary shortage of gold in the vault. Later, central banks came to formalise this process by gathering all gold reserves under a single institution in order to prevent temporary shortage of liquidity in a particular bank. The same basic principles still apply to the banking system with the difference that cash roughly plays the role that was historically that of gold, while electronic credit plays the historical role of the physical banknote. Another difference is that the monetary base, which previously was made up of gold, is currently based on debt bonds.

---

43 See for example David Astle, *Babylonian Woe: A Study of the Origin of Certain Banking Practices*, 1975 (self-published).

2.3 General Dynamics of Interest

In his *Politics*, Aristotle made a distinction between management of resources and the art of getting rich, which is the classical line of difference between the respective fields of economics and chrematistics.[44] Frederick Soddy (see chapter 1.3) mentions philosopher John Ruskin's perspective on chrematistics as being the art of getting rich in relation to others, so that those with less became the dependent servants (slaves) of those with more.[45] Historically, a central part of chrematistics was usury. Today, usury means to use someone's naivety, distress or dependency for your own gain, or to charge a very high level of interest on a loan. The ancient Greeks denoted the very practice of charging interest as usury, regardless of the interest level. Aristotle condemned interest because he considered it deeply contrary to nature and argued that money should only function as a means of exchange.[46] What is it with interest that has brought about such strong standpoints throughout history? On the one hand, interest encourages a borrower to repay debts quickly and compensates the lender for refraining from using the money over a period of time and risking that the loan will not be repaid. On the other hand, interest also entails chrematistic tendencies. Kathrin Latsch of the Monetary Network Alliance estimates that interest income and costs on a social level causes a redistribution of wealth from 80 per cent of the population to the wealthiest 10 per cent, while a tenth of the people has as much interest income as they have interest costs.[47] Cause and effect between the parts and the whole can be more

---

44 Aristotle, *Politics*, book 1, part 8–10.

45 Article by Frederick Soddy, *Cartesian Economics: The Bearing of Physical Science upon State Stewardship*, London, 1921, p. 7.

46 Aristotle, *Politics*, book 1, part 10.

47 See Monetary Network Alliances at Monneta.org, the video *A Flaw in The Monetary System?* by Kathrin Latsch, http://vimeo.com/71074210 as of May 31, 2016. According to personal correspondence between Latsch and the author, a Ralf Becker at University of Manchester calculates the interest costs.

lucidly illustrated if they are viewed in a simplified and exaggerated scale. Using a fictive scenario to cartoon the general dynamics of the interest mechanism in the current banking and monetary system is a good way of understanding it. Imagine a closed mini-economy in which 10 people are granted interest-bearing loans from one person who is the only source of credit (money). The creditor is a greedy usurer who grants credits with an interest level of 50 per cent, which must be paid each year — or else he has the right to redeem the collateral given in exchange for the credit. Nevertheless, all 10 people take a loan of $100,000 each to build a house, which is also given as collateral together with the lot they are built on. Altogether, the money supply is $1,000,000 but given that no new loans are granted it is a matter of time — two years at most — before all of the $1,000,000 should be paid back to the usurer as interest. If no one is granted another loan and thus contributes to the economy with new money, all real estates will end up in the hands of the usurer when the collaterals must be redeemed, as no one can afford to pay the interest. While this process is completed, the 10 people will fight to find money to pay the interest and the loans. Bernard Lietaer describes the dynamic like this:

> Money is created when banks lend it into existence. When a bank provides you with a $100,000 mortgage, it creates only the principal, which you spend and which then circulates in the economy. The bank expects you to pay back $200,000 over the next 20 years, but it doesn't create the second $100,000 — the interest. Instead, the bank sends you out into the tough world to battle against everybody else to bring back the second $100,000.[48]

To bring the example to a head, one might imagine that the usurer, after the 10 economic actors have given up their collateral and no longer

---

48 *Beyond Greed and Scarcity*, article in *Yes! Magazine*, interview with Bernard Lietaer, http://www.yesmagazine.org/issues/money-print-your-own/beyond-greed-and-scarcity as of May 31, 2016.

have any possessions, grants them all new loans in a new round. In exchange, the usurer then demands that the borrowers give the only resource they can offer as collateral—their services. If they cannot repay the loans they can work away the interest, at $10 an hour, by building a palace for the usurer. Given that no new loans are granted, the borrowers will altogether have to work 50,000 hours a year on building the palace to compensate for their failure to pay the interest, which on a collective plane is impossible to pay. In this fictive example, the building of the palace illustrates the conditions given in order to be granted a loan or to pay interest on an existing loan. Theoretically, these conditions can assume any form decided by the creditor and which the borrower agrees on in the contract, including digging a hole and filling it up again, or, if it applies to a state, make changes in their policies. In reality, credit grants can include harsh conditions, which the deals between the troika (EU, ECB and IMF) and Greece are one example of. This dynamic is very a real process and a consequence of the current design of the monetary system. The outcome is a continuous flow of goods and service production to creditors, mainly commercial banks, from the rest of the economy. In reality, the process is slower than in the example of the usurer above but the basic principles are the same. The economy expands in times when credit is granted plentifully. When the credit tap is closed, the consequence is deflation and accumulation of collateral to creditors through a process similar to the game of musical chairs, in which more and more participants lack a chair—or in more concrete wording are not able to pay their interest and debt.

One might take our cartooned example and instead imagine that the 10 borrowers act in an open economy with other actors using the same currency. In this scenario, the borrowers have two options—either they earn new money in the surrounding economy in order to repay the interest and the principal, or they will be forced to surrender their collateral. In other words a growth pressure arises because of the interest and the debt. The borrowers have to produce and sell more goods and services in the surrounding economy to be able to repay the interest and their loans. Let us assume that all borrowers, after a number of years, manage to repay their loans by making a total $5,000,000 in the surrounding economy. The usurer might then lend out this $5,000,000 with the same interest rate to another 50 people and the cycle is repeated once again. With time, there is an ongoing concentration to the usurer, which is compensated with collateral if he does not get the money back or with financial growth if the borrowers manage to repay their debts.

Since all money in a debt-based monetary system is created as interest-bearing debt, there will never be enough money to repay all debt and interest. New loans must continuously be granted if the economy is to keep going and for every loan an even bigger sum of money must be returned. The alternative is credit contraction and debt cancellation against different forms of compensation, such as selling of collateral. A debt-based monetary system leads to accumulation of economic resources to the credit system as a whole in the form of money (in booms) and/or resources in the form of collateral (in downturns), and a growth pressure because of a set condition of scarcity in which there is always more debt than available money in circulation. Another consequence of this dynamic is that the hidden interest costs in consumer prices become high. Kathrin Latsch estimates that such costs on average amount to 30 per cent of consumer prices in goods and services.[49]

2.4 Financial Rulership Techniques

New complexity research shows that financial institutions have socioeconomic influence in ways other than impacting the monetary

---

49 See note 47.

supply in either direction by granting more or fewer loans. A study published in 2011 — *The Network of Global Corporate Control*[50] by three Swiss economists at Swiss Federal Institute of Technology in Zurich — showed that 40 per cent of the total market value of all the world's transnational corporations is concentrated on a core that is made up of 147 bodies, out of which three-quarters are financial institutions, and has almost complete control over itself. In other words, this core makes up a joint consortium, which through a complex network of ownership exercises directs hierarchical control over a significant part of the global economy.

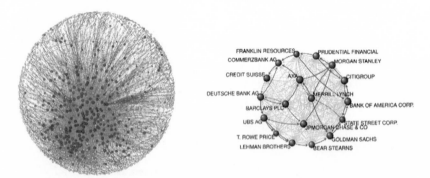

Figure 3. According to Glattfelder et al, control of the world economy is highly concentrated on financial institutions through indirect and direct shareholding.

Judging by a letter from Franklin D. Roosevelt, President of the U.S. from 1933 to 1945, that was addressed to colonel Edward Mandell House and dated 1933, it has long been an established fact that the tentacles of Wall Street reach all the way into politics:

> The real truth of the matter is, as you and I know, that a financial ele-
> ment in the larger centers has owned the government ever since the days
> of Andrew Jackson — and I am not wholly excepting the administra-

50 *The Network of Global Corporate Control*, Stefania Vitali, James B. Glattfelder and Stefano Battiston, ETH Zürich, 2011.

tion of Woodrow Wilson. The country is going through a repetition of Jackson's fight with the Bank of the United States — only on a far bigger and broader basis.[51]

One might note that Roosevelt accentuates that the political control of big finance was not a result of the introduction of the Federal Reserve System in 1913, under the reign of Woodrow Wilson's administration, even though it was deepened at that point. According to Roosevelt's letter, the fight for power over monetary policy has been going on at least since the administration of Andrew Jackson, between 1829 and 1837. Carrol Quigley, a history professor at Georgetown University, maintains that some of the combatants have had a far-reaching aim to dominate not only the American political system but the political systems of *all* countries and the global economy as a whole. In the preface of *Tragedy and Hope* (1966), Quigley writes:

> The powers of financial capitalism had another far-reaching aim, nothing less than to create a world system of financial control in private hands able to dominate the political system of each country and the economy of the world as a whole. This system was to be controlled in a feudalistic fashion by the central banks of the world acting in concert, by secret agreements arrived at in frequent private meetings and conferences. The apex of the system was to be the Bank for International Settlements in Basel, Switzerland, a private bank owned and controlled by the world's central banks, which were themselves private corporations. Each central bank... sought to dominate its government by its ability to control Treasury loans, to manipulate foreign exchanges, to influence the level of economic activity in the country, and to influence cooperative politicians by subsequent economic rewards in the business world.[52]

---

51 *F.D.R.: His Personal Letters, 1928–1945*, edited by Elliott Roosevelt, 1950, Duell, Sloan and Pearce, New York, p. 373.

52 Carrol Quigley, *Tragedy & Hope*, first published in 1966 by The Macmillan Company, New York, foreword.

Quigley's words are especially credible considering his close contact with the political and financial establishment. As a mentor for Bill Clinton, he got a personal mention at the Democratic convention when Clinton was named as the party's presidential candidate in the White House race of 1992.

The description of how meetings between chairmen of central banks at the Bank for International Settlements affect the world economy is exemplified by the Basel Accords. Basel III is being gradually implemented up to 2019 and, for example, brings about more capital regulation for commercial banks — which, all other things being equal, will result in a decreased money supply as a consequence of a lessened multiplier effect. OECD has estimated the negative effect of Basel III on GDP at between 0.05 and 0.15 per cent annually.[53] Another example of financial rulership techniques that Quigley mentions is big loans that can be recalled with short notice and thus give creditors the possibility of exercising direct or indirect blackmail on borrowers. Considerable power is also concentrated in the three dominating credit-rating agencies — Moody's, Standard & Poor's and Fitch — which by a degradation of creditworthiness can dip any nation or corporation into economic crisis. For example, a small country like Finland would suffer from much tougher conditions following a downgraded credit rating, as the market would demand higher interest rates for Finnish government bonds. This was exactly what happened in the case of Greece in the aftermath of the latest financial crisis. John Perkins, author of *Confessions of an Economic Hitman* (2005), tells of more Wild West-like variants of how financial and political power can merge. The following excerpt is from an interview in which Perkins talks about his experiences as a so-called economic hitman on the news show *Democracy Now*:

---

53 OECD Library, http://www.oecd-ilibrary.org/economics/macroeconomic-impact-of-basel-iii_5kghwnhkkjs8-en as of May 31, 2016.

[We] economic hitmen, basically in the last four decades, have managed to create the world's first truly global empire [...] We've done it primarily without the military. The military comes in only as a last resort. We've done it through economics, and we've done it very, very subtly, so it's been a secret empire, unlike all of history's previous empires. [...]

And the way economic hitmen work, we use many different techniques, but probably the most typical is that we'll identify a company [country] that has resources that corporations covet, like oil. We'll arrange a huge loan from an organization like the World Bank for that country; but the money won't go to that country at all. It goes to big U.S. corporations — Bechtel, Haliburton, ones we all hear about all the time — to build infrastructure projects in that country.

These projects, like industrial parks and power plants, benefit the very rich of those countries and do nothing for the poor, except to leave the country in a huge debt, one it can't possibly repay, which means it can't give social services, education, health to its poor, and it's put in a position where it doesn't repay its debts; so, at some point, we economic hitmen go back in and we say: 'Look, you can't repay your debts, so give us a pound of flesh. Sell oil to our oil companies real cheap or vote with us at the next U.N. vote, or send troops in support of ours some place in the world.' And that's how we've created this empire; and we've done it without most Americans even realizing that it's happening.[54]

In the same interview, Perkins says Omar Torrijos, the president of Panama, was murdered in 1981 because he refused to follow directions from economic hitmen.

Mass media is another means of power that can be used to influence the development of society. In 1917, U.S. congressman Oscar Callaway alleged that J. P. Morgan was buying a dominant position on the media market:

---

54 Interview with John Perkins on *Democracy Now*, March 3, 2006, http://www. democracynow.org/2006/1/3/former_economic_hit_man_john_perkins as of May 31, 2016.

In March, 1915, the J. P. Morgan interests, the steel, shipbuilding, and powder interest, and their subsidiary organizations, got together 12 men high up in the newspaper world and employed them to select the most influential newspapers in the United States, a sufficient number of them to control generally the policy of the daily press of the United States. [...] They found it was only necessary to purchase the control of 25 of the greatest newspapers. The 25 papers were agreed upon; emissaries were sent to purchase the policy, national and international; [...] an editor was furnished for each paper to properly supervise and edit information regarding the questions of preparedness, militarism, financial policies, and other things of national and international nature considered vital to the interests of the purchasers. [...] The policy also included the suppression of everything in opposition to the wishes of the interests served.[55]

In *The Underground History of American Education: A Schoolteacher's Intimate Investigation Into the Problem of Modern Schooling* (2000), John Taylor Gatto makes a case that trust funds such as the Rockefeller Foundation have played an influential role in general social development by, among other things, processing the educational system.[56]

Following the leads Quigley gave, one can also find support to suggest that big finance makes use of different types of semi-anonymous forums for collaboration to discuss working topics with business leaders and politicians. According to Quigley's information, the British mining magnate and politician Cecil Rhodes bequeathed the majority of his fortune from mining in Rhodesia (now Zimbabwe and Zambia) and the Cape Colony to establish an anonymous organisation with the aim of promoting the development of global hegemony under British

---

55 Article in *The New Work Times*, February 14, 1917, *For Press Investigation*, http://query.nytimes.com/gst/abstract.html?res=9504E7DA1538EE32A25757C1A9649C946696D6CF as of May 31, 2016.

56 John Taylor Gatto, *The Underground History of American Education*, 2000–2001, Oxford Village Press, Oxford.

control.[57] Nathan Rothschild is named in *Tragedy and Hope* as one of the figures Rhodes contemplated as being a member of the organisation's inner circle. In *Rothschild: A Story of Wealth and Power* (1988), which Derek Wilson wrote in collaboration with the Rothschild family, who gave him access to a substantial part of their archives, it is confirmed that Rhodes wrote a will in 1888 which, according to Nathan Rothschild, would administer the main part of his wealth to finance an omnipotent secret society working for the advancement of British imperial power.[58] The background to this act ought to have been, among other things, that Rothschild provided financial support for Rhodes' Africa project. According to Quigley, Rhodes' will laid the groundwork for what came to be the Round Table, an octopus organisation out of which groups including the Council on Foreign Relations (CFR) was developed, as an arm with a specific focus on America. On the CFR website, J. P. Morgan Chase & Co, Bank of America, Citigroup and Goldman Sachs, among others, are listed as founders. In the so-called President's Circle can be found Barclays, Bloomberg, Credit Suisse, Deutsche Bank, Moody's, Morgan Stanley, Soros Fund Management, Shell and Google. Rothschild North America Incorporated is listed among its corporate members together with Standard & Poor's, PwC, Western Union, Microsoft, Facebook, AT&T, Time Warner, Merck, GlaxoSmithKline and Walmart. Prominent personal CFR members within the financial sector have, for example, included Paul Warburg (chairman of the CFR from 1921 to 1933 and a participant in the Jekyll Island meeting of 1910), David Rockefeller (board member of the CFR from 1949 to 1985, chairman 1970 to 1985), Paul Volcker (chairman of the Federal Reserve 1979 to 1987), Alan Greenspan (ditto, 1987 to 2006), James Wolfensohn (head of the World Bank 1995 to 2005), Paul

---

57 Quigley, pp. 130–132.

58 Derek Wilson, *Rothschild: a story of wealth and power*, Andre Deautsch, Storbritannien, 1988. Taken from the Swedish version *Rothschild: Familjen, makten, rikedomen*, 1988, Gedin, Stockholm, p. 219.

Wolfowitz (ditto, 2005 to 2007), Robert Zoellick (ditto, 2007 to 2012) and the financial magnate George Soros. Among the more well-known CFR politicians are the American presidents George H. W. Bush and Bill Clinton.[59] In the fall of 2013, Danish media brought attention to a study by Dino Knudsen of Copenhagen University on how the CFR-akin Trilateral Commission, a forum whose main focus is Asia, has influenced Western governments for more than 40 years.[60] The members of the CFR and the Trilateral Commission overlap some-what — for example, long-time CFR chairman David Rockefeller is the founder of the Trilateral Commission.[61]

The same Rockefeller is also a member of the Bilderberg Group, which is primarily focused on Europe. Wolfowitz, Wolfensohn and Zoellick are other examples of prominent CFR members who have participated in Bilderberg conferences.[62] From a Nordic angle, we can mention Jorma Ollila (the former CEO of Nokia) and Jacob Wallenberg, who have both operated as members of the Bilderberg steering committee for many years. With the background information brought out in this chapter, there ought to be enough ground to il-lustrate a pyramid of power of financial and political capital along the lines of figure 4.

---

59 Council on Foreign Relations roster, http://www.cfr.org/about/corporate/roster. html, http://www.cfr.org/about/membership/roster.html, http://www.cfr.org/about/history/cfr/appendix.html as of January 11, 2015.

60 *Lukket elitært netværk har i 40 år påvirket regeringar,* article on Danmarks Radio November 5, 2013, http://www.dr.dk/Nyheder/Udland/2013/11/04/200554.htm as of May 31, 2016.

61 Trilateral Commission on David Rockefeller, http://trilateral.org/go.cfm?do=Page.View&pid=21 as of January 10, 2015.

62 Bilderbergmeetings — list of participants, http://www.bilderbergmeetings.org/participants_2011.html, http://www.bilderbergmeetings.org/participants_2010. html, http://www.bilderbergmeetings.org/participants_2008.htmlhttp://www. bilderbergmeetings.org/steering-committee.html, http://www.bilderbergmeet-ings.org/former-steering-committee-members.html as of January 10, 2015.

Economists know that the free market is a hypothetical ideal that rarely or never exists in its purest form but the question is whether one generally realises to what degree financial and political power today are overlapping and concentrated on a macrosocial level. The current structures of the banking and monetary system make up a central platform for such concentration of power to be upheld and strengthened. Against that background, the discussion in the third chapter focuses on different aspects of alternative monetary systems and monetary reforms.

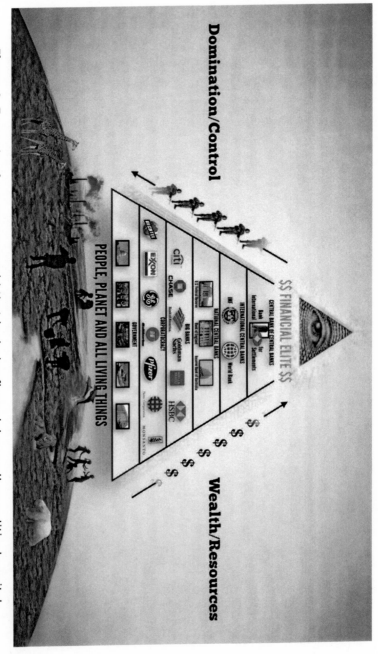

Figure 4. Example of a power pyramid that includes financial as well as political capital.

3. Alternative Monetary Systems

For a state to say that it cannot realise its objectives
because there is no money
is the same as saying that one cannot build roads
because there are no kilometres.

EZRA POUND[63]

There are, to put it mildly, very different opinions on how the monetary system should be reformed. Some even think that money in itself is an evil and for that reason want to abolish the monetary system altogether. The focus of this third chapter is to show different aspects of alternative monetary systems, which can differ depending on how a specific system is designed. At least seven such aspects, listed on the following page, can be distinguished.

---

63 The quote is attributed to Ezra Pound. It is a paraphrase of parts of his article *What Is Money For* (1935), in which Pound also mentions that he is not the original inventor of this metaphor without specifying where he got it.

1) Control. Who has control over the creation of money? What agenda are those in control serving? What principles are consequently applied in regulating the monetary system and the monetary supply?

2) Reserves. Should the banking system be based on fractional or full reserves? This is indirectly connected to the first aspect because fractional reserve banking means banks can create money when they issue loans. Full reserve banking means that banks cannot lend money without the permission of the depositor and thus cannot create money by granting credit.

3) Convertibility. Should a currency be tied to, for example, gold? Should it be a fiat currency, which is not tied to a certain quantity of a specific good or service?

4) The interest mechanism. Should the interest mechanism keep the same role it has today? Should all interest be viewed as usury? Should it be something in-between, for example by making the process under which new money is issued interest-free?

5) Integrity and transparency. Should the aim of a currency be to monitor all transactions or to maximise personal integrity and make anonymous transactions possible? Is the banking and monetary system easy to understand for the public and thus transparent from the point of view of scrutiny?

6) Monoculture or multiculture. Should one strive to have a single currency in a society or should there be monetary diversity on a global and national level?

7) Goal function. The goal function refers to the aggregate purpose (whether it is articulated or not) of a certain monetary and banking system. All of the above mentioned aspects are based on the goal function for what a certain system strives to accomplish and can be adapted to the specific conditions in a specific society.

3.1 Control

The control of the banking and monetary system can be centralised to a single institution or distributed among several institutions. The most basic aspect of this control is regulation of money supply, including its creation and destruction. John Maynard Keynes argued that inflow of new money does not cause a general rise of the price level as long as there is untapped production capacity because of low purchasing power. However, Keynes did not put as much focus on *how* such influx would come about. There is a crucial difference between money being issued as interest-bearing debt to commercial agents, as is the case today, compared with an institution issuing it by buying goods and services on behalf of the public without commercial banks as intermediaries. The inventor Thomas Edison was perhaps an unexpected advocate public reform according to this principle, notably in an interview with *The New York Times* in December 1921:

> If our nation can issue a dollar bond, it can issue a dollar bill. The element that makes the bond good, makes the bill good, also. The difference between the bond and the bill is the bond lets money brokers collect twice the amount of the bond and an additional 20%, whereas the currency pays nobody but those who directly contribute to [society] in some useful way. ... It is absurd to say our country can issue $30 million in bonds and not $30 million in currency. Both are promises to pay, but one promise fattens the usurers and the other helps the people.[64]

There is reason to suppose that the most central public projects can be financed by spending new money into circulation, rather than lending it into circulation as is done today. Even if the purchasing power is already maximised, and new money thereby causes a general rise in the price level instead of increasing productivity, one might accept a minor annual rise in the general price level, of for example two per cent, as a form of indirect taxation. Certain investments can potentially

---

64 *Ford Sees Wealth in Muscle Shoals*, article in *The New York Times*, July 16, 1922.

also give returns that can be recirculated into the economy, whereupon it is paid back — for example, a new energy plant that charges a fee for electricity. Such investments consequently do not affect the monetary supply over the whole process.

An alternative way to spend currency into circulation by public purchases is so-called social credit, formulated in C. H. Douglas' *Social Credit* of 1924[65], which suggests that the state issues new currency directly into citizens' wallets as a form of basic income. In certain contexts, currency spent into circulation through the public budget is referred to as 'Greenbacks', named after the special form of dollars with a green backside that were issued by Abraham Lincoln's administration to finance the Union forces in the American Civil War.[66] An example of a monetary system in which the state spends money into circulation, rather than first borrowing and then spending it into circulation like today, can be found even further back in history. Tally sticks operated as legal tender in medieval England. The tallies were decorated pieces of wood broken into two matching parts. One half was spent into circulation by the royal power and was accepted as tax payment. As all pieces were broken in a unique way, the tallies were hard to counterfeit and fraud was detected at the latest when the tally was returned to the issuer. The tally currency functioned as means of exchange until a gold standard succeeded it after the introduction of

65 Clifford Huge Douglas, *Social Credit*, first published in 1924, Gordon Press, New York.

66 Contemporary legal experts, economists and historians, have interpreted the extensive legislation surrounding the Greenbacks in various ways. Legislation and stenographed discussion on the theme is archived in the Library of Congress, see for example House of Representatives Bill 240 from 1862, http://memory. loc.gov/cgi-bin/ampage?collId=llhb&fileName=037/llhb037.db&recNum=1096 as of May 31, 2016.

the Bank of England in 1694.[67] According to Thorold Rogers, a 19th century economist and historian from Oxford, by the end of the 15th century an ordinary peasant or worker in England could provide food for his family for a year by working between 10 and 15 weeks.[68] Such a number indicates that the economic system of the time functioned well for the broader public, which should be possible to ascribe at least partly to the tally currency.

The hyperinflation in the Weimar Republic between 1920 and 1923 has been used as a warning of why it is not a good idea for the state to control the money machine. However, Hjalmar Schacht, director of the Reichsbank in the Weimar Republic between 1923 and 1931, and in Nazi Germany between 1933 and 1939, testified about aspects of the German economy in those periods that are generally not mentioned in modern textbooks. In his book *The Magic of Money*, published three years before his death in 1970, Schacht mentions that loans granted by the Reichsbank for private speculation in the early 1920s were a contributing factor to the runaway inflation.[69] Furthermore, Schachts offers a complementary explanation to how following Adolf Hitler's rise to power in 1933, Germany was able to recover from economic ruin and mass unemployment in such a short time and become Europe's leading industrial nation, with full employment. The economic recovery in 1930s Germany is especially spectacular considering that it took place during the Great Depression, a time in which the rest of the world suffered severe economic hardship. Some point towards the discontinued payments of the war indemnities imposed under the Treaty

---

67 See for example *Talliess and Technologies — Monetary innovation goes back a long way*, Dave Birch, 2002, http://www.thocp.net/timeline/papers/tallies.pdf as of May 31, 2016.

68 James E. Thorold Rogers, *Six Centuries of Work and Wages: The History of English Labour*, 1884, republished by Batoche Books, Kitchener, 2001, p. 388, available on http://socserv2.socsci.mcmaster.ca/econ/ugcm/3ll3/rogers/sixcenturies.pdf as of May 31, 2016.

69 Hjalmar Schacht, *The Magic of Money*, 1967, Oldbourne, London, p. 70.

of Versailles as a contributing factor while others have supposed that it was made possible by the confiscation of Jewish-owned assets. Foreign investment and support from the Bank for International Settlements have also been mentioned as possible variables in the equation. According to Schacht, the primary factor was the implementation of the MEFO bills that the state, in cooperation with the Reichsbank, started to inject into the economy soon after Hitler's takeover:

> The MEFO system was a noteworthy example of the fact that it is possible to make up for a lack of capital by means of credit without any risk of engendering an inflation that causes price rises. [...] The English economist J. M. Keynes has dealt with the problem theoretically, and the MEFO transactions proved the practical applicability of such an idea.[70]

Schacht describes the design of the MEFO system as follows:

> The system worked in the following way: a company with a paid-up capital of one million marks was formed. A quarter of the capital was subscribed by each of the four firms Siemens, A. G. Gutehoffunungshiitte, Rheinstahl and Krupps. Suppliers who fulfilled state orders drew up bills of exchange for their goods, and these bills were accepted by the company [as payment]. This company was given the registered title of Metallforschungsgesellschaft (Metal Research Company, 'MEFO' for short), and for this reason the bills drawn on it were called MEFO bills. The Reich guaranteed all obligations entered into by MEFO, and thus also guaranteed the MEFO bills in full. [...]
>
> One other aspect was even more unusual. The Reichsbank undertook to accept all MEFO bills at all times, irrespective of their size, number, and due date, and change them into money. The bills were discounted at a uniform rate of four per cent. By these means the MEFO bills were almost given the character of money, and interest-carrying money at that. Banks, savings banks, and firms could hold them in their safes exactly as if they were cash.[71]

---

70 Ibid p. 116.

71 Ibid p. 113.

With these words, Schacht recognised the success of the MEFO bills. At the same time, in the final years of his leadership, he did not want to advance the system in the way that the highest state leadership wished for. Schacht claims that this was the reason why he was forced to abandon his post in January 1939.[72] In *Mein Kampf* (1925) it appears Hitler had strong personal opinions on banking and monetary policy. In chapter 8, titled *Beginnings of My Political Activity*, Hitler writes that the monetary question became part of his political platform as early as 1919, thanks to a Gottfried Feder:

> When listening to Gottfried Feder's first lecture about the breaking of the tyranny of interest, I knew immediately that the question involved was a theoretical truth that would reach enormous importance for the German people's future. [...] Germany's development already stood before my eyes too clearly for me not to know that the hardest battle had to be fought, not against hostile nations, but rather against international capital. [...] The fight against international finance and loan capital has become the most important point in the program of the German nation's fight for its independence and freedom.[73]

Along with Anton Drexler, Feder was one of the Nazi Party's earliest key personalities. As its leading economic ideologue, Feder formulated, among other things, the party's plans for the decisive elections in 1932 and 1933. Besides the anti-Semitic features, the party programme states of its economic principle on page 30: 'Finance shall exist for the benefit of the state; the financial magnates shall not form a state within the state. Hence our aim to break the thraldom of interest.' In more concrete terms, it is advocated that the state should abolish its debts to the great financial houses, issue interest-free currency to finance public projects and establish a bank in order to grant interest-free loans

---

72 Ibid p. 117.

73 Adolf Hitler, *Mein Kampf*, Chapter 8 — *Beginnings of my political activity*, English version published in 1941 by Reynal & Hitchcock, New Work, p. 287. First published by Fritz Eher Verlag, Munich, 1925.

for business development.[74] Schacht, who was not a National Socialist, opposed several of these reforms and also seems to have managed to ward them off during his leadership. Schacht writes in *The Magic of Money*:

> National Socialist agitation under the leadership of Gottfried Feder was directed in great fury against private banking and against the entire currency system. Nationalisation of the banks, liberation from the bondage of interest, the introduction of a state 'Feder' giro money, these were the catchphrases by which an end was to be made to our monetary and banking economy. I had to try to steer Hitler away from these destructive conceptions.[75]

Schacht's statement, together with his background in the international financial sector, makes it seem curious that upon the National Socialists taking power Feder only got a marginal position in the new government while Schacht was appointed president of the Reichsbank and minister of economics. Even though Schacht's MEFO bills saved the country in the short-term they were emitted, if Schacht's description is correct, as an interest-bearing debt according to principles that are very similar to the dynamics of the modern monetary system. One of several possible explanations for the appointment of Schacht rather than Feder is his earlier experience and that it was part of alliance building with industrial interests, among which Schacht was far more popular than the more populistically-focused Feder. Despite the tragedies that this epoch brought with it, one can conclude that it constitutes a remarkable chapter in monetary history that shines further light on the great political drama that has surrounded the control of the banking and monetary system.

---

74 Gottfried Feder (1932), *The Program of the NSDAP — The National Socialist German Workers' Party and its General Conceptions*, p. 30, published in English in 1980 by B. P. Publication, Shotton, United Kingdom. First published by Fritz Eher Verlag, Munich, 1932.

75 Schacht p. 154–155.

Options for reforms intended to raise awareness of money power as a central social instrument of power include acknowledging it as a fourth independent power alongside the legislative, executive and judicial, and introducing general elections for a chief executive or a board of governors to oversee this power. One might also emphasise that money power does not necessarily have to be a public institution. It can also be controlled by a non-profit organisation or commons trusts, according to Peter Barnes' description in *Capitalism 3.0.*[76] The Wikimedia Foundation is one example of how such commons trusts can be used, in that case to manage the non-profit encyclopedia Wikipedia. Theoretically, it is possible to build a currency commons using the same principle. Local Exchange Trading Systems, or LETS, offer many examples of how such currency commons can be designed on a local level. LETS first developed in the 1980s in Courtenay, Canada — a town blighted by an unemployment level of around 40 per cent. Having noticeably improved the situation, the local population embraced the new currency and it has since spread over the whole world in many variations.[77] The name of a specific currency can vary and LETS is just a common denominator for the basic idea of constructing a currency commons under local, regional, national or potentially even under global control. A business-to-business variation of a LETS-like system is the Swiss currency WIR, which has operated on a national level in parallel with conventional currency and has helped stabilise the Swiss economy since 1934.

---

76 Peter Barnes, *Capitalism 3.0: A guide to reclaiming the commons,* 2006, Berrett-Koehler Publishers, San Francisco.

77 Lietaer and Dunne, p. 75.

According to a study from 2010, the WIR was used by 16 per cent of all Swiss companies.[78] A typical LETS scheme gives every person in a currency commons (geographical or with another common denominator for its users) the right to a certain amount of interest-free credit, which they can use to buy goods and services. For example, a person can go to the hairdresser and agree to pay, let's say, €5 and L15. The customer's LETS account is then debited with -L15 while the hairdresser is credited +L15 for the service. In this moment, new money gets created. The amount of credit every person is allowed to create, and the rules applied to grant credit, can be designed freely depending on the needs and goals of the society in question.

3.2 Reserves

In order for money creation to be shifted from private to public or other common control, the current system based on fractional reserves must be reformed into a system based on what is called full reserves. Fractional reserve banking also makes the system vulnerable. This is because problematic situations can arise if a certain amount of depositors decide to withdraw their money from the bank or cannot meet their loan obligations. The International Monetary Fund counts the number of financial crises between 1970 and 2010 at 425, which splits as 145 banking crises, 208 currency crises and 72 national debt crises.[79]

---

78 *Rethinking Money*, article on *Huffington Post* by Jacqui Dunne, December 9, 2012, http://www.huffingtonpost.com/jacqui-dunne/rethinking-money_b_2268797. html as of May 31, 2016. See also the profile of WIR at Community Currency Knowledge Gateway, http://community-currency.info/en/currencies/wir-bank/ as of May 31, 2016.

79 IMF Working paper: *Resolution of Banking Crises: The good the bad and the ugly* by Luc Laeven and Fabian Valencia, http://www.imf.org/external/pubs/ft/ wp/2010/wp10146.pdf as of May 31, 2016.

Of these, at least the banking crises are interlinked with the fragility
built into systems based on fractional reserves.

Regarding financial stability, it is also worth mentioning the big insurance companies. When the financial crisis of 2008 set in, it was not
only banks that needed extra support to avoid collapse. Big insurance
companies such as AIG were also in need of rescue packages, in large
part because of Credit Default Swaps (CDS), which in the aftermath of
the crisis became known as financial weapons of mass destruction. In
practice, CDS is an equivalent in the insurance business of fractional
reserve banking, in the sense that they originate from insurance companies making far greater commitments than they can carry out in
times of financial crisis.

A reform designed to prevent such financial crises is the Chicago
Plan, which was presented as early as 1933 at the University of Chicago.
Its authors took inspiration from Frederick Soddy's work in an attempt
to reform the American economy during the Great Depression. IMF
economist Michael Kumhof, mentioned in the second chapter, is
among those who have brought up the plan in a modernised version.[80]
In general terms, the Chicago plan entails a transition to the system
many people mistakenly believe is already in place — that banks can
only lend money they get from deposits. After such a reform, lending
would demand the permission of the depositor, which means the depositor cannot demand the money back while the money is lent out for
the simple reason that both lender and borrower are very aware that
the money is lent out. With such a reform, bank runs would no longer
be a potential problem as all the money available on the customer's
account, in a system based on full reserves, must always be in the bank.
Another consequence of this reform is that depositors can more easily
control the ways in which their money is used. Under the Chicago

---

80 IMF Working Paper: *The Chicago Plan Revisited* by Jaromir Benes and Michael
Kumhof, http://www.imf.org/external/pubs/ft/wp/2012/wp12202.pdf as of May
31, 2016.

Plan seigniorage, which is the profit from creating new money, would be transferred from commercial banks to the public. The proposal by Chicago-inspired IMF economists has a strong resemblance to a proposal by British think-tank Positive Money.[81]

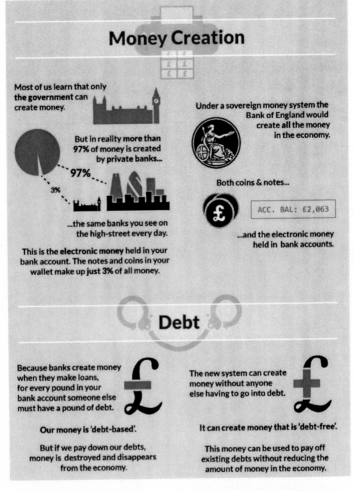

Figure 5. Parts of the proposal from Positive Money.

---

81 Summarised in *Modernising Money: Why Our Monetary System is Broken and How it Can be Fixed*, Jackson and Dyson (2012), published by Positive Money, United Kingdom.

Positive Money's vision includes a transition to full reserves by distinguishing deposit accounts, in which money is simply stored, and accounts for lending and investment. Furthermore, the proposal advocates, among other things, allowing money creation to be controlled by an independent and democratically elected committee, which would decide on the amount of money to be added into the economy while the government would be responsible for the spending of the money. Such a system differs from the current central banking system in that new money is injected into the real economy first, rather than today's entry via mortgage loans and purchasing various security papers on the financial markets, which only indirectly stimulates the real economy. These measures aim to decrease the risk of housing market bubbles and stimulate employment more effectively.

Soddy's suggestion on how a transition to full reserves could be implemented without causing financial meltdown, which is the danger if the process is handled carelessly, was to let banks lend new money from the state bank to cover their reserve deficits. With this maneuver, the banks would retain their liquidity without having to recall loans and public debt would be decreased, settled or turn into a demand. Viewed in the context of fractional versus full reserves, the Single Resolution Mechanism under which the European Banking Union's member countries have a collective responsibility to rescue failing banks is thus a solution focusing on the symptoms and not on the underlying causes of the current instability of the financial system.

3.3 Convertibility

The 2011 movie *In Time* is a literal portrayal of the expression that time is money. It is set in a world in which people stop ageing when they turn 25. Everyone has a ticking clock on their arm and if it ticks down to zero, it automatically executes them using an implanted microchip. Everyone gets paid for goods and services in hours, days and weeks. The rich live for ever while the poor, in a very concrete sense, live day by day. In such a reality, one might conclude that the demand for this currency is guaranteed because of its intimate relationship with time. The currency Ithaca HOURS[82], one of the most circulated currencies in the U.S., is a less extreme variation of a time-based currency established on a general guideline that one HOUR equals one hour of work. However, the guideline is not mandatory and anyone can pay extra for more demanding services. In Japan, the time-based currency Fureai Kippu ('care relation ticket') has been used to complement elderly care. Assistance for the ageing population is paid for with a currency that can be used during one's own illness or pension, or can be given to relatives in need of care in other parts of the country.[83] To make a currency directly convertible to time, gold or some other good or service is to aim to guarantee the exchange value of a currency and trust in it, both in the short and long-term. The most typical example is the gold standard, which means you can redeem paper money for gold. To some extent, one might say that the U.S. dollar is still indirectly backed by the petrodollar, which has meant it has only been possible to buy oil for dollars. The guaranteed global demand for oil has in return guaranteed demand for dollars. One might speculate as

---

82   Article on Ithaca Hours' founder Paul Glover, *Ithaca Hours revival would require community support,* http://www.ithaca.com/news/ithaca-hours-revival-would-require-community-support/article_175100c4-65d6-11e0-bd73-001cc4c002e0. html as of May 31, 2016.

83   Community Currency Knowledge Gateway, http://community-currency.info/en/currencies/asia/fureai-kippu/ as of May 31, 2016.

to whether Iran's decision to leave this dollar standard and instead sell oil in exchange for other currencies such as the yen, yuan and rouble has been an underlying motive for America's hardline political stance in relation to the country.

A proposal brought up for discussion in Russia is to make a transition from the petrodollar by tying the rouble to an electric standard, which would guarantee a certain amount of kilowatt-hours in exchange for a rouble.[84] Vladimir Zaznobin, a professor of conceptual technology (see chapter 1.7) from Saint Petersburg Agrarian University, is one of the idea's proponents. Zaznobin argues that the move would make economics more scientific through the establishment of a defined unit of measurement for economic value that corresponds with the metric unit and other units in the natural sciences. An advantage of the electro standard in contrast to the petrodollar, according to the reasoning of Zaznobin, is that it can be defined in more exact terms. He claims the advantage of the gold standard was what he calls an invariant price list — a term he uses to denote a good or service that all other goods and services in the rest of the economy is measured by, be that gold or kilowatt-hours. Zaznobin concludes that gold has played this role historically but a gold-based currency can no longer serve the needs of modern civilisation because of its weak real-world ties to the modern economy. Electricity, however, is one of its most basic prerequisites. One might suppose that a new currency based on an electro standard would reasonably only be issued when the production of electricity increases. If increased production of electricity allows increased capacity for industrial production, it ought to be possible to issue new electro currency without causing a rise in the general price level. One might further suppose that the control of currency creation under an electro

---

84 Article by Vladimir Zaznobin in New Europe, *EU, Russia, Secure Future For Europe,* http://www.neurope.eu/article/eu-russia-secure-future-europe as of May 31, 2016.

standard is affected by who controls and regulates the production of electricity.

Carbon-based currency is also, to some extent, a sort of energy standard in a society that is dependent on fossil fuels. A great risk with carbon currency, however, is the possibility of the permitted emissions, and thus the money supply, being tightened without compensating with an equivalent extension of energy resource replacement, thereby causing economic meltdown.

Bernard Lietaer's suggestion for a global reference currency, called Terra[85], is an example of how a currency can be backed in a more diversified manner. The Terra system is developed to work as a complementary currency in global trade, aiming to support the economy especially in times of low economic activity. The Terra system, illustrated in figure 6, can be described in the following five steps:

1a: An oil producer, with an excess inventory of 1 million barrels of oil, sells that quantity to the Terra alliance.

1b & 1c: The Terra alliance sells some of that oil to increase its holdings of the other 11 component commodities backing the currency. The commodities are supposed to be those most used in global trade such as copper, grain or claims to container transport.

1d: The alliance credits the Terra account of the oil producer with a quantity of Terra units equal to the current purchasing power of 1 million barrels of oil. If the market price of oil is, let us say, $100 per barrel and Terra is set with a reference price of $10, the oil is bought for 10 million Terra. This is when new Terra gets created.

---

85   Article by Bernard Lietaer and Gwendolyn Hallsmith in *The Solutions Journal —
     Making Money For Business: Currencies, Profit and Long-Term Thinking*, http://
     www.thesolutionsjournal.com/node/992 as of May 31, 2016.

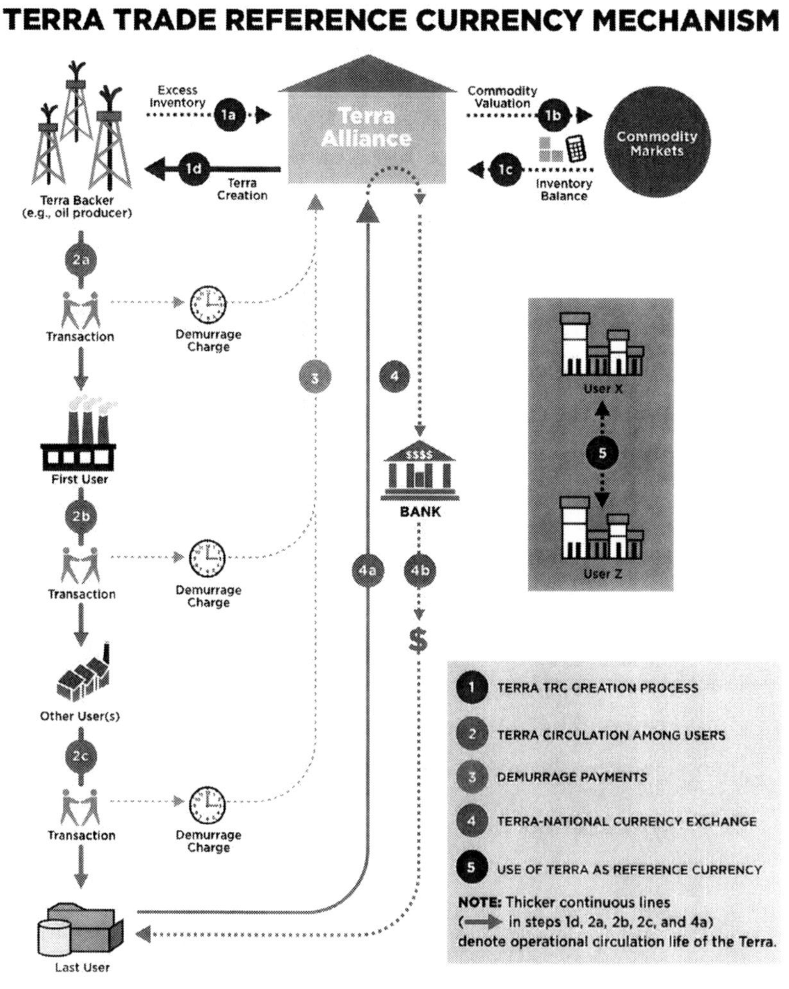

TERRA TRADE REFERENCE CURRENCY MECHANISM

Figure 6. Scheme of the Terra currency.

2a: The oil producer uses the Terras to buy an oil rig from a company willing to accept the Terras in trade.

2b: The rig supplier uses the Terras to buy components from its own suppliers.

2c: The process continues with the Terras circulating until redeemed.

3: The oil producer and other Terra users pay a so-called demurrage charge when using the Terra, based on how long the Terra was held in their accounts. If the demurrage charge is set to 1 per cent per year and an account owner has had 100,000 Terra on the account on average, 1,000 Terra is charged from the account. The fee is used by the Terra alliance to finance the administration of the currency. The other purpose of the fee is to encourage continued circulation of the currency. The main function of the Terra is thus primarily to be a means of exchange and only secondarily to function as a store of value.

4: Whenever Terras are redeemed, the final user is charged a 2 per cent redemption fee. The purpose of the fee is to make it more favorable to keep the currency in circulation rather than redeeming it. If the currency is redeemed, the alliance first sells the commodities corresponding to the redeemed Terras on the open market and then pays the redeeming party in conventional currency.

5: Piggybackers can also use the Terra as a trade reference currency, pricing contracts in it but settling those contracts in an equivalent amount of another currency. This decreases the risk for loss as a result of currency fluctuations.

Besides complementing the economic cycle, the purpose of the Terra is to make it easier for companies to operate without loans and thereby counteract short-term thinking and artificially conditioned growth pressure as a consequence of interest-bearing debt. Companies and even countries can sell excess commodities in exchange for Terra. The currency is designed to work in parallel with conventional currency and only exists electronically. As for the currency's backing, one can see that the Terra is convertible to a varied basket of commodities.

In the discussion about backing, one can also mention that conventional money keeps its value in three ways. First, one must have such money to pay tax. Second, there is always a larger amount of debt than there is available money. Third, there is always a need for a tool that can function as a means of exchange, a store of value and a standardised measure of value. This means that a fiat monopoly, which is not specifically backed by any particular good or service (such as electricity), is in fact backed by the aggregated production of goods and services — or as Soddy put it, by the virtual wealth.

At worst, guaranteed convertibility to a certain amount of a specific good can be damaging to the economy. A gold standard guarantees that money can be converted to a certain amount of gold but it supposes that increases in productivity are compensated by price deflation instead of an increased currency supply and stable price levels. Proponents of the gold standard often argue that a gold-based currency would be superior when it comes to the stability of the currency — but the volatility of the gold price suggests that not even this aspect can be taken for granted. In addition, the ability to store value is not necessarily the most central aspect of a functioning monetary system, which is demonstrated by the Wörgl experiment examined in the next chapter. When investigating whether a monetary system should be based on convertibility to a certain commodity or not, one must consequently specify what the aim of such backing is. Different conditions in different economies can demand different solutions to accomplish the wished-for result.

3.4 The Interest Mechanism

An old story tells of a Persian emperor who was so excited about the new game of chess that he offered to grant its inventor any wish. The inventor was a very clever mathematician and asked for one grain for the first square on the board, two grains for the second and a doubling amount on each of the remaining squares. The emperor was at first very happy at the apparent modesty of the mathematician, until he realised that this exponential growth would demand that he gave him more grain than was available in the whole world, only to satisfy the amount of grain asked for in the last square.

Perhaps it is such exponential dynamics on compound interest that led Aristotle and the prophets of the old Middle East to clearly articulate how one is supposed to use and lend money in accordance with the higher natural order.

It is stated in the Koran that trade is not contrary to God's will. However, interest (referred to as usury) is categorically condemned:

> Those who eat usury (Riba) will not stand (on the Day of Resurrection) except like the standing of a person beaten by Satan leading him to insanity. That is because they say 'Trading is only like usury,' whereas Allah has permitted trading and forbidden usury. So whosoever receives an admonition from his Lord and stops eating usury shall not be punished for the past; his case is for Allah (to judge); but whoever returns to usury, such are the dwellers of the Fire — they will abide therein.[86]

In the Old Testament, Deuteronomy presents a markedly different approach that shows the perspective on loans and interest as mechanisms of social control is very old:

> For the Lord your God will bless you, as he promised you, and you shall lend to many nations, but you shall not borrow, and you shall rule over many nations, but they shall not rule over you. [...]

> You shall not charge interest on loans to your brother, interest on money, interest on food, interest on anything that is lent for interest. You may charge a foreigner interest, but you may not charge your brother inter-

---

86 The Koran, 2 Al-Baqarah, 275, http://www.noblequran.com/translation/ as of May 31, 2016.

est, that the Lord your God may bless you in all that you undertake in the land that you are entering to take possession of it.[87]

With such diametrically opposed take-off points as those above, it's understandable that the interest issue has been a contributing factor to tensions between the Abrahamic religions. Jesus was, at least based on the New Testament, not as explicit in this regard as were Moses and Muhammad. Nevertheless, one might note that the only time Jesus is said to have been violent was when he drove the money changers out of the temple and accused them of having made it into a den of robbers.[88] This Biblical episode might have been a contributing ideological factor to the temporary restrictions regarding interest applied by the Catholic Church.

A general moral objection to interest is that it provides a profit for the creditor without production of a good or service. The systemic challenge for an interest-free banking and monetary system, as is advocated by the Koran, is to find functioning substitutes to the advantages of interest such as incentives to lend money and repay loans. JAK Member bank in Sweden has developed its own solution to this by demanding a certain amount of saving before, during and after the borrowing period as a counter-performance to the granting of credit. The monthly costs of the loan are about the same as the costs of an ordinary bank loan but the difference is that a borrower at JAK, after paying off the loan, has saved a considerable amount of capital they can then freely dispose of. Besides completely interest-free models such as JAK, there are other modern alternatives for reforming the role of the interest mechanism in the societal order. Ellen Brown suggests that interest should finance the costs of the public and uses a vivid fiction to illustrate this:

---

87 Deuteronomy, 15:6, 23:19–20, English Standard Version.

88 Mentioned several times in the New Testament, see for example Mark 11:15–19.

The Wicked Witch of the West rules over a dark fiefdom with a single private bank owned by the Witch. The bank issues and lends all the money in the realm, charging an interest rate of 10 per cent. The Witch prints 100 witch-dollars, lends them to her constituents and demands 110 back. The people don't have the extra 10, so the Witch creates 10 more on her books and lends them as well. The money supply must continually increase to cover the interest, which winds up in the Witch's private coffers. She gets progressively richer, as the people slip further into debt. She uses her accumulated profits to buy things she wants. She is particularly fond of little thatched houses and shops, of which she has an increasingly large collection. To fund the operations of her fiefdom, she taxes the people heavily, adding to their financial burdens.

Glinda the Good Witch of the South runs her realm in a more people-friendly way. All of the money in the land is issued and lent by a 'people's bank' operated for their benefit. She begins by creating 110 people's-dollars. She lends 100 of these dollars at 10 per cent interest and spends the extra 10 dollars into the community on schemes designed to improve the general welfare — things such as pensions for retirees, social services, infrastructure, education and research and development. The $110 circulates in the community and comes back to the people's bank as principal and interest on its loans. Glinda again lends $100 of this money into the community and spends the other $10 on public schemes, supplying the interest for the next round of loans while providing the people with jobs and benefits. For many years, she just recycles the same $110, without creating new money. [...] Best of all, taxes are unknown in the realm.[89]

An example of a government owning its own commercial bank, with the possibility to grant credit and use interest income for public purposes, is the Bank of North Dakota, which has been active in the state of the same name since 1919. A political objection to public ownership of banks (or other types of ownership such as commons trusts) is that it is a type of socialism or communism not suited to a modern market economy. However, if interest profits are used to fully or partly replace

---

89 Ellen Brown, *The Web of Debt*, 2008, Third Millennium Press, Los Angeles, p. 409.

taxation, one can argue that there is also a capitalistic aspect that is as essential as the socialistic aspect of public ownership of banks. One can also conclude that concepts such as socialism and capitalism are not always used in a consistent manner in the political debate. One example of this is that buy-ups financed by the public can be referred to as 'socialistic threats' while bailouts financed in exactly the same way (e.g. during and after the financial crisis of 2008) can be referred to as 'a prerequisite for capitalism'. An alternative to both buy-ups and bailouts is to issue future rescue packages to failing financial institutions as loan packages and thereby compensate the public with an interest-bearing claim on the banks in question.

The Chicago Plan and the reform proposals by Positive Money mentioned in chapter 3.2, under which money is created only by a public institution while a commercial bank would still be allowed to lend against interest, are in this context more moderate alternatives that can possibly lessen the negative effects of interest on a macro level.

When discussing interest mechanism reform, we must finally mention demurrage fees, which may be viewed as a form of negative interest. Demurrage is not negative interest in the sense that one gets paid to borrow money but that one pays a fee to hold money. The earlier analysis of Terra is a theoretical example of such a set-up. The most famous practical example of a monetary system based on demurrage fees is the Austrian currency Wörgl, which was used in a small town of the same name in 1932.[90] In 1931, the mayor of the town, Michael Unterguggenberger, was in a desperate economic situation in the aftermath of the Great Depression and convinced the town's administration to test the principles laid out by the German economist Silvio Gesell in his book *The Natural Economic Order* (1918). The experiment was based on a currency with a monthly demurrage fee of one per cent.

---

90 Unterguggenberger Institut Wörgl, *The Monetary Experiment In Wörgl — Wörgls Free Money*, article by Veronika Spielbichler, translated by Christian Lechner, http://www.unterguggenberger.org/getfile.php?id=4983 as of May 31, 2016.

The fee was represented with stamps, which could be bought in local shops and were put on matured notes at the end of each month.

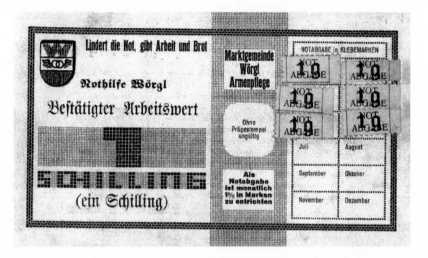

Figure 7. Wörgl currency from 1932 with stamps affixed as receipts for the paid usage fee.

The experiment was ended abruptly after just over a year, when the central government issued a ban on continued the use of the currency. In a letter in which Unterguggenberger himself summarises the experiment, he expressed a great disappointment over the halt as he had noted a remarkable improvement in the local economy, in the form of lower unemployment and healthier public finances due to the higher rate of circulation of the currency that the fee resulted in.[91] Demurrage differs from inflation and a consequential rise in the general price level in that the general price level can be held stable over time while, because of lost purchasing power, the costs of individual actors are predictable and transparent. The theoretical basis of demurrage fees is that the primary function of money is to be a means of exchange

---

91 Personal letter by Michael Unterguggenberger translated by G. Spiller, http:// monetary-freedom.net/reinventingmoney/unterguggenberger-end_results_of_worgl_experiment.html as of May 31, 2016. Original source: Annals of Collective Economy, Geneve, Schweiz 1934.

and its role as a store of value is complementary but secondary. Margit Kennedy compares money's function as a medium of exchange with a railway carriage serving as a medium for the transport of goods, with the rent for using the monetary infrastructure being reasonable in the same way as that demanded for the use of railway infrastructure.[92] Henry Ford had a similar idea when he argued that the monetary system should be viewed as an actual part of the transportation system:

> The function of money is not to make money but to move goods. Money is only one part of our transportation system. It moves goods from man to man. A dollar bill is like a postage stamp; it is no good unless it will move commodities between persons.[93]

Gresham's law states that money that is losing value will be used as a means of payment before money that keeps its value. If a classical gold-based currency could hypothetically circulate in parallel (see chapter 3.5) with a currency such as Wörgl, it is likely that the Wörgl currency would dominate trade. Further, the demurrage system has an inbuilt incentive to lend money interest-free. This is because lending such a currency makes the lender avoid the fee — a dynamic that makes it possible to keep the interest level at zero per cent. Furthermore, demurrage encourages advance payments, which in fact constitutes a form of interest-free credit (for the vendor) and saving (for the buyer). The income from the fee also makes it possible to finance the administration of the system and may furthermore finance a certain amount of public expenses. Together with initiatives such as JAK and North Dakota, the experience from Wörgl shows that the interest mechanism can be adapted in various ways, with different consequences for the economy.

---

92 Margit Kennedy, *Interest and Inflation Free Money*, 1995, Seva International, p. 13.

93 Robert L. Owen, *National Economy and the Banking System*, 1939, United States Government Printing Office, Washington p. 101.

3.5 Monoculture or Multiculture

Lietaer presents an original perspective on money by asking whether it is necessary for a single currency to fulfil all functions as a means of exchange, standard of measure and store of value. A demurrage currency, the foremost function of which is a means of exchange, could, for example, be complemented with silver and gold, which would function as a store of value. Are there benefits of using parallel currencies with specialised qualities for different purposes? An advantage, according to Lietaer, is that the resilience of the economic system would be strengthened. In the same way as biological monocultures are more sensitive to change than ecosystems with a higher degree of diversity, Lietaer argues that monetary monocultures are less resistant to stress than an economic system with several currencies existing in parallel.[94] Friedrich Hayek touched upon Lietaer's way of reasoning when he wrote about the modern currency monopoly in the following way:

> It is an extraordinary truth that competing [parallel] currencies have until quite recently never been seriously examined. [...] [The monetary monopoly] has the defects of all monopolies: one must use their product even if it is unsatisfactory, and, above all, it prevents the discovery of better methods of satisfying a need for which a monopolist has no incentive.[95]

The point Hayek makes is that a currency monopoly makes it harder to determine whether the specific type of money being used is the most suitable to fulfil its functions, as there are no other currencies to compare it with. However, one can conclude to some extent that parallel currencies already exist, something that has been shown in previous

---

94 Lietaer and Dunne, p. 33.

95 Friedrich Hayek (first print, 1976), *Denationalisation of Money: The Argument Redefined. The Theory and Practice of Concurrent Currencies*, The Institute of Economic Affairs, p. 28.

chapters. Lietaer estimates the amount of complementary currencies in the world today to be around 4,000.[96] Bonus points awarded by airline companies are in some regards another example of a parallel currency, with companies issuing their own form of credit for marketing purposes. In times of low economic activity in particular, when a greater amount of goods and services remain unused, there might be a social gain from using such complementary currencies. A currency monopoly has the advantage that it does not need backing as money is always in demand as a tool to manage virtual wealth. In a system with several currencies working in parallel, it is probably somewhat harder for a particular fiat currency to guarantee its status. It might thus be the case that the need for confidence-promoting mechanisms through convertibility is greater in a monetary multiculture than in a monoculture. Something that should be mentioned in this discussion are the legal conditions for parallel, alternative currencies, which differ from country to country. In general, they are not illegal. The concept of legal tender can be confusing and does not generally mean that it is the only legal means of payment but that the public and companies are obligated to accept legal tender as a payment of debts, goods and services *if nothing else has been agreed upon*.[97] The fact that bank credit today makes up more than 90 per cent of the monetary supply and that bank credit, for example according to Swedish law, does not constitute legal tender (only coins and notes are considered legal tender in Sweden) shows that there is a creative space for other actors to create currency beyond what is deemed legal tender.

---

96 Article on Forbes by Peter Ferrara, March 1, 2013, http://www.forbes.com/sites/peterferrara/2013/03/01/rethinking-money-the-rise-of-hayeks-private-competing-currencies/#1a7e05a72f56 as of May 31, 2016.

97 Swedish Nationalencyklopedin, keyword 'lagligt betalningsmedel' ('legal tender' in Swedish), http://www.ne.se/lang/lagligt-betalningsmedel as of March 8, 2014.

3.6 Integrity and Transparency

The Western world has traditionally viewed the tendency of totalitarian regimes in the former Eastern bloc to read citizens' mail as a severe infringement on human dignity. However, as of today it has become a fully normalised practice to systematically store and monitor digital correspondence in democratic nations — and monetary transactions are no exception. In light of this situation, it is relevant to briefly mention integrity and transparency as a separate aspect in the discussion on currency reform. Integrity in this context refers to protected information, while transparency refers to just that — whether the system is transparent or not. The question is *to whom* a currency system is transparent and *what type* of information it protects. The current system is transparent to the political and financial central administration. However, for the average user it is not, because among other things very few individuals understand how the system works. Alternative currencies such as Wörgl differ in this regard because their simple design is more easily understood and thereby transparent from the perspective of users and scrutinisers.

So-called cryptocurrency is also relevant to the discussion about integrity and transparency, because it makes anonymous monetary transactions possible. Bitcoin, a cryptocurrency created by someone using the pseudonym Satoshi Nakamoto, has had a lot of media attention over the past few years and brought the concept of cryptocurrency to the awareness of the general public. As encrypted digital currency has the potential to challenge the very foundations on which the current currency and tax systems stand, it is understandable that governments generally associate Bitcoin with the great risks of hacking, black markets and money laundering. For example, the director of Bank of Finland, Erkki Liikanen, has highlighted the absence of a central controlling third party in monetary transactions as a general weakness of Bitcoin.[98] In contrast with conventional digital transactions made in the current banking system, transactions with Bitcoin take place directly between vendors and buyers with digital software as the only intermediary. From the perspective of users, one can also conclude that Liikanen is right in that Bitcoin brought with it certain risks, such as its drastic change in value both up and down, and with the hacking in 2014 of the Bitcoin exchange Mount Gox. Another question mark regarding Bitcoin is whether the monetary programming of the currency, with gradually decreasing growth of the monetary supply, is adapted to the needs of the real economy in the event that it is increasingly used as a means of exchange. In a hypothetical scenario in which Bitcoin outcompetes conventional currency, it is possible that banking based on fractional reserves might become necessary to contribute an extra flexibility that the programmed increase of the money supply lacks. Optimists believe Bitcoin and other cryptocurrencies will be improved over time and compensate for weaknesses in their current programming. One thing is certain though — Bitcoin has fuelled discussion about what money is and what it could be. Cryptocurrency demonstrates that programmers can create monetary systems with characteristics that can potentially revolutionise the economic and social order. At the moment, there are many different digital currencies and it remains to be seen whether Bitcoin or some other cryptocurrency can contribute to a monetary paradigm shift.

3.7 Goal Function

The goal function of the monetary system is not to be confused with the goals of the central bank, such as, for example, price stability or

---

98 Lecture by Erkki Liikanen at Ålands Lyceum, September 29, 2014 where the author was present. An excerpt can be viewed at https://www.youtube.com/watch?v=VYrsS834mxQ, film published on YouTube by Anders Casén at Ålands Lyceum.

full employment. This is because the central bank only makes up one aspect of the banking and monetary system. The goal function describes the purpose of the monetary system as a whole, whether it is explicitly stated or not. Viewed as a whole, the current system is in practice, even though it is not explicit, based on what can be described as a chrematistic goal function by which financial and (indirectly) political capital is concentrated to financial institutions. On the one hand, the goal function is a more general aspect that can seem less concrete than the previously mentioned aspects. On the other hand, one should bear in mind that the goal function makes up the basic foundation that the six previously mentioned aspects must be based upon. The systems presented in the third chapter are mainly based on goal functions that have a common denominator in that they strive for the monetary system to serve the interests of the public rather than to make the public serve a financial elite, with a money flow that meets the potential supply of goods and services or, according to Soddy's terminology, the virtual wealth. In such systems, the aggregated capacity of the economy does not depend on whether there is enough money or not but on access to human capital and raw materials. It is from this perspective that one should read the quote from Ezra Pound's article *What Is Money For*, which opened this chapter:

> For a state to say that it cannot realise its objectives
> because there is no money
> is the same as saying that one cannot build roads
> because there are no kilometres.

Francis Bacon is said to have coined the phrase that money is a good servant but a bad master, which is a good summary of a chrematistic goal function that accumulates capital to an elite, in contrast with an alternative goal function that serves the interests of the public.

Epilogue

Based on what has been presented in this book, it should be evident that there are dimensions of the monetary field that have to a large extent been neglected in science, media and politics. In the discussion it has been shown that money power can be viewed as a social management tool, just as with the executive, legislative and judicial powers. From this perspective, it can be noted that the discrepancy between different banking and monetary systems is as significant as that between radically different political systems.

The current monetary system furthers centralisation of economic and political power to a financial elite, which has been possible because the system is difficult to grasp not only for the masses but also for the so-called intellectual elite. Because banks, money and debt have generally been viewed as fringe issues without any importance to economic and social development, economists have not put enough attention on exploring the field from new perspectives that can give a better understanding of the properties of money power.

A perspective that can offer new possibilities for analyzing different types of monetary systems and their socio-economic consequences is to view economics as an energy science analogous to electrics and mechanics. Based on the document *Silent Weapons for Quiet Wars*, money can be viewed as potential economic energy moving in the opposite direction of goods and service production, which in turn correspond to dissipative and kinetic energy respectively. Compared with conventional theoretical frameworks such as the quantity theory, the energy theory implicitly makes it clear that it is not enough (although necessary) to take into account money supply and speed of circulation in order to understand fluctuations in price and production, and that tendencies in the monetary flow must also be taken into account.

An example of how an analysis of monetary flows can contribute with more clarity is the way in which quantitative easing (QE) by central banks can exist in parallel with low price inflation or even deflation. A model such as the quantity theory does not catch up that QE is issued by buying obligations that primarily affect the stock market rather than the real economy.

Conventional models also overlook to a large extent the way in which economic actors are indebted to each other and how these relations affect power relationships in different sectors of society. The current situation in which individuals, corporations and whole nations have been put in a position of dependency in relation to global finance could most probably not go on for very long if economists established new standard models that exposed this dynamic. A related area that could benefit from flow-based analysis is how the flow of interest income and expenditure affects private and public actors, and whether negative interest systems such as, for example, that of Wörgl can give rise to a different dynamic.

The author's ambition with this work is not to suggest an all-encompassing monetary solution on a national and international level but it is highly desirable that other economists eventually respond to that challenge. However, regarding potential solutions, one can conclude that several of the alternative monetary systems presented in the third chapter have a common denominator in that they do not let the banking and monetary system automatically serve the interests of a specific group of people or institutions and instead put it in service of the public interest. One might add that alternative monetary systems have different characteristics and different types of economies can make use of this by adapting the respective aspects of a monetary system such as control, convertibility and interest (in a classical sense or negative interest in the form of demurrage), depending on the conditions of the economy in question. The increasing number of cryptocurrencies in the wake of Bitcoin, together with the increased use of parallel local currencies, could be an early sign of an impending monetary revolution that might eventually change the financial system in a way similar to the internet's impact on the media landscape, even if change proves to be impossible to make from a political level. Economists are therefore urged to prepare for such a scenario by putting a greater focus on the monetary question.

The author hopes that this book can encourage other researchers to pick up and further clarify the dynamics of the current system, including its political consequences, and explore which alternative systems are most appropriate from national, regional and international perspectives. Hopefully, the study of money power can continue in the spirit of Frederick Soddy, whose words from 1934 neatly sum up what should be the fundamental purpose of continued research and its application:

> Let us not enslave men that pretenders may rule, but take back our sovereign powers over money in order that men can be free.[99]

---

99 Soddy, *The Role of Money*, p. 219.

Sources

Figures

1) A basic model of economic flows available in many standard text books.

2) Model by Mike Maloney, hiddensecretsofmoney.com as of May 31, 2016.

3) Illustration from *The network of global corporate control* by Stefania Vitali, James B. Glattfelder and Stefano Battista.

4) Model by Foster Gamble, http://www.thrivemovement.com/images/infographics/followthemoney.html as of January 11, 2015.

5) Reform proposal by Positive Money, http://www.positivemoney.org/our-proposals/debt-based-money-vs-sovereign-money-infographic/ as of May 31, 2016.

6) Model by Bernard Lietaer, http://www.thesolutionsjournal.com/node/992 as of May 31, 2016.

7) Wikipedia, keyword 'Wörgl', http://en.wikipedia.org/wiki/W%C3%B6rgl as of January 11, 2015.

Literature

Aristotle, *Politics*, book 1.

Astle, David, *Babylonian Woe: A Study of the Origin of Certain Banking Practices*, 1975, self-published.

Barnes Peter, *Capitalism 3.0: A guide to reclaiming the commons*, 2006, Berrett-Koehler Publishers, San Francisco.

Bordo, Michael D. and Roberds, William, *A Return to Jekyll Island — The Origins, History and Future of the Federal Reserve*, 2013, Cambridge University Press, Cambridge.

Brown, Ellen, *The Web of Debt*, 2008, Third Millennium Press, Los Angeles.

Douglas, C. H., *Social Credit*, 1924, Gordon Press, New York.

Fisher, Irving, *100 % Money*, 1935, republished in 1996 by Pickering and Chatto Publishers, London.

Ford, Henry, *My Life and Work*, 1922, Doubleday, Page & Company, New York.

Galbraith, John Kenneth, *Money: Whence it came, where it went*, 1975, republished in 2001, Houghton Mifflin Books, Boston.

Gatto, John Taylor, *The Underground History of American Education*, 2000–2001, Oxford Village Press, Oxford.

Gesell, Silvio, *The Natural Economic* Order, first published in German in 1916 with the title *Die natürliche Wirtschaftsordnung durch Freiland und Freigeld*, published in a revised edition in 1956 by Peter Owen Publishers, London.

Griffin, Edward G., *The Creature from Jekyll Island*, 1994, American Media, California.

Hayek, Friedrich, *Denationalisation of Money: The Argument Redefined. The Theory And Practice of Concurrent Currencies*, 1976, The Institute of Economic Affairs, London.

Hitler, Adolf, *Mein Kampf*, 1925, Fritz Eher Verlag, Munich.

Jackson, Andrew and Ben Dyson, *Modernising Money: Why Our Monetary System is Broken and How it Can be Fixed*, 2012, Positive Money, United Kingdom.

Jevons, William Stanley, *Money and The Mechanism of Exchange*, 1875, D. Appleton and Co, New York.

Kennedy, Margrit, *Interest and Inflation Free Money*, 1995, Seva International, Michigan.

Lietaer, Bernard and Dunne, Jacqui, *Rethinking Money — How New Currencies Turn Scarcity Into Prosperity*, 2013, Berrett-Koehler Publishers, San Francisco.

Owen, Robert L., *National Economy and the Banking System*, 1939, United States Government Printing Office, Washington.

Patman, Wright, *A Primer on Money*, 1964, United States Government Printing Office, Washington.

Perkins, John, *Confessions of an Economic Hitman*, 2005, Plume/Penguin Books, New York.

Rand, Ayn, *Atlas Shrugged*, 1957, Random House, New York.

Roosevelt, Elliott, *F. D. R. : His Personal Letters 1928–1945*, 1950, Duell, Sloan and Pearce, New York.

Rothboard, Murray, *Making Economic Sense*, 1995, Ludwig von Mises Institute, Alabama.

Schacht, Hjalmar, *The Magic of Money*, 1967, Oldbourne, London.

Soddy, Frederick, *The Role of Money*, 1934, George Routledge and Sons, London.

Solonko, Igor, *Fenomen Kontseptualnoj Vlasti: Sotsialno-Filosofskij Analiz* (Феномен Концептуальной Власти: Социально-Философский Анализ), 2010, Solo, Saint Petersburg.

Smith, Adam, *The Wealth of Nations*, 1776, republished in 1904 by Methuen & Co, London.

Thorold, Rogers James E., *Six Centuries of Work and Wages: The History of English Labour*, 1884, republished in 2001 by Batoche Books, Kitchener, Canada.

Quigley, Carrol, *Tragedy & Hope*, 1966, The Macmillan Company, New York.

Warburg, Paul, *The Federal Reserve System: Its Origin and Growth*, 1930, Macmillan, New York.

Wilson, Derek, *Rothschild: Familjen, makten, rikedomen*, 1988, Gedin, Stockholm, original title: *Rothschild: A story of wealth and power*, Andre Deautsch, UK, 1988.

Other sources

The Bible, Deuteronomy, Gospel of Mark.

Bank of Finland, press release nr 11, March 24, 2014, http://www.suomenpankki.fi/sv/suomen_pankki/ajankohtaista/tiedotteet/pages/tiedote11_2014.aspx as of May 31, 2016.

Bilderberg meetings, participants and members of the steering committee, http://www.bilderbergmeetings.org/participants_2011.html, http://www.bilderbergmeetings.org/participants_2010.html, http://www.bilderbergmeetings.org/participants_2008.html, http://www.bilderbergmeetings.org/steering-committee.html, http://www.bilderbergmeetings.org/former-steering-committee-members.html as of January 10, 2015.

Bloomberg Businessweek, 'Company Lookup', keyword 'Bank of Finland' etc., http://investing.businessweek.com/research/common/symbollookup/symbollookup.asp?lookuptype=private&region=all&textIn=Bank%20of%20FInland as of January 11, 2015.

Birch, Dave, *Tallies and Technologies — Monetary innovation goes back a long way*, article written for History of Computing Foundation, 2002, http://www.thocp.net/timeline/papers/tallies.pdf as of May 31, 2016.

Boman, Isac, *Nätverksekonomi*, Bachelor's thesis, Åbo Akademi, 2011, Turku.

Community Currency Knowledge Gateway, profile of the WIR and the Fureai Kippu, http://community-currency.info/en/currencies/wir-bank/ as of May 31, 2016.

http://community-currency.info/en/currencies/asia/fureai-kippu as of May 31, 2016.

Council on Foreign Relations, membership roster from CFR, http://www.cfr.org/about/corporate/roster.html, http://www.cfr.org/about/membership/roster.html, http://www.cfr.org/about/history/cfr/appendix.html as of January 11, 2015.

Dunne, Jacqui, *Rethinking Money*, article in *Huffington Post*, December 9, 2012, http://www.huffingtonpost.com/jacqui-dunne/rethinking-money_b_2268797.html as of May 31, 2016.

Encyclopedia of Marxism, keyword 'capital', http://marxists.org/glossary/terms/c/a.htm#capital as of January 2, 2015.

Feder, Gottfried, *The Program of the NSDAP: The National Socialist German Workers' Party and its General Conceptions*, 1932, Fritz Eher Verlag, Munich, 1932, published in English in 1980 by B. P. Publication, Shotton, Storbritannien.

Federal Reserve, FAQ, http://www.federalreserve.gov/faqs/about_14986.htm as of May 31, 2016.

Federal Reserve Bank of Chicago, *Modern Money Mechanics — A Workbook on Bank Reserves and Deposit Expansion*, first published in 1961 by Federal Reserve Bank of Chicago Public Information Center, available on the web in an updated version from 1994.

Ferrara, Peter, *Rethinking Money: The Rise Of Hayek's Private Competing Currencies*, article in *Forbes*, March 1, 2013, http://www.forbes.com/sites/peterferrara/2013/03/01/rethinking-money-the-rise-of-hayeks-private-competing-currencies/ as of May 31, 2016.

Finlex, Law on Bank of Finland, http://www.finlex.fi/sv/laki/ajanta-sa/1998/19980214 as of May 31, 2016.

Finnish Body of Law, state budget of 2013, http://www.edilex.fi/data/sdliite/
liite/6165.pdf as of May 31, 2016.

Finnish Government, public debt administration, structure of the government debt, http://www.treasuryfinland.fi/sv-FI/Statistik/Statsskuld/
Statsskuldens_struktur as of May 31, 2016.

Glattfelder, James B., Vitali Stefania, Battiston Stefano, *The network of global
corporate control*, 2011, ETH Zürich.

Grace Commission, *The President's Private Sector Survey on Cost Control*,
January 12, 1984, The Library of Congress, Congressional Research
Service, US.

Government Printing Office, p. 12, http://digital.library.unt.edu/ark:/67531/
metacrs9044/m1/1/high_res_d/IP0281G.pdf as of May 31, 2016.

Ithaca.com, Article about Ithaca Hours' founder Paul Glover, *Ithaca
Hours revival would require community support*, http://www.ithaca.
com/news/ithaca-hours-revival-would-require-community-support/
article_175100c4-65d6-11e0-bd73-001cc4c002e0.html as of May 31, 2016.

Kumhof, Michael and Benes, Jaromir, *The Chicago Plan Revisited*, IMF
Working Paper published on IMF's webpage, http://www.imf.org/exter-
nal/pubs/ft/wp/2012/wp12202.pdf as of May 31, 2016.

Latsch, Kathrin, video published on Monetary Network Alliance — monneta.
org: A flaw in The Monetary System?, http://vimeo.com/71074210 as of
May 31, 2016.

Laeven, Luc and Valencia, Fabian, *Resolution of Banking Crises: The good
the bad and the ugly*, IMF Working paper: http://www.imf.org/external/
pubs/ft/wp/2010/wp10146.pdf as of May 31, 2016.

Lewis, John L., Federal Court Decision: 680 F.2d 1239 (1982), https://law.
resource.org/pub/us/case/reporter/F2/680/680.F2d.1239.80-5905.html as
of May 31, 2016.

Lietaer, Bernard, *Beyond Greed and Scarcity*, article in *Yes! Magazine*, http://www.yesmagazine.org/issues/money-print-your-own/beyond-greed-and-scarcity as of May 31, 2016.

Making Money For Business: Currencies, Profit and Long-Term Thinking, article written together with Gwendolyn Hallsmith in *The Solutions Journal*, http://www.thesolutionsjournal.com/node/992 as of May 31, 2016.

Liikanen, Erkki, lecture at Ålands Lyceum, September 29, 2014 at which the author was present. An excerpt can be viewed at https://www.youtube.com/watch?v=VYrsS834mxQ, film published by Anders Casén at Ålands Lyceum.

Maloney, Mike, *Hidden Secrets of Money* part 4 (video), http://hiddensecretsofmoney.com/videos/episode-4 as of May 31, 2016.

Nationalencyklopedin, keyword 'kapital', http://www.ne.se/kapital as of November 24, 2014, keyword 'legal tender', http://www.ne.se/lang/lagligtbetalningsmedel as of March 8, 2014.

New Work Federal Reserve, overview of Member Banks, *Second District Member Banks* at http://www.newyorkfed.org/banks.html as of May 31, 2016.

OECD Library, report on the impact of Basel III, http://www.oecd-ilibrary.org/economics/macroeconomic-impact-of-basel-iii_5kghwnhkkjs8-en as of May 31, 2016.

Pedersen, Falkentoft Jan, *Lukket elitært netværk har i 40 år påvirket regeringar*, article on *Denmark Radio*, November 5, 2013, http://www.dr.dk/Nyheder/Udland/2013/11/04/200554.htm as of May 31, 2016.

Perkins, John, interview on *Democracy Now*, March 3, 2006, http://www.democracynow.org/2006/1/3/former_economic_hit_man_john_perkins as of May 31, 2016.

Pound, Ezra, *What Is Money For*, article, 1935, https://archive.org/details/WhatIsMoneyFor as of May 31, 2016.

Pujo Committee Report, investigation led by Arséne Pujo on behalf of the US Congress (Report of the Committee Appointed Pursuant to House

Resolutions 429 and 504: 1912–1913 — Pujo Committee Report). Available on http://www.scribd.com/doc/34121180/Pujo-Committee-Report-Report-of-the-Committee-Appointed-Pursuant-to-House-Resolutions-429-and-504-1912-1913-Pujo-Committee-Report as of May 31, 2016.

Riksbanken (Swedish National Bank), letter to Henning Witte, http://files.meetup.com/189080/riksbanken%20svar%20pdf%208.7.10.pdf as of May 31, 2016.

Soddy, Frederick, *Cartesian Economics: The Bearing of Physical Science upon State Stewardship* (article), 1921, London.

Spielbichler, Veronika, *The Monetary Experiment In Wörgl — Wörgls Free Money*, article written for Unterguggenberger Institut Wörgl, translated by Christian Lechner, http://www.unterguggenberger.org/getfile.php?id=4983 as of May 31, 2016.

Sveriges Television / *Vetenskapens Värld: Den ekonomiska vetenskapen*, documentary pruduced by *Vetenskapens Värld* (Swedish Public Service), broadcasted on november 19th, 2012. Available on youtube.com with English Subtitles as of May 31st 2016 — 'Economic Science and the Debt Crisis (*Vetenskapens Värld* 19-11-2012)'.

The New York Times — Ford Sees Wealth in Muscle Shoals, article in *The New York Times*, July 16, 1922. Oscar Callaway is quoted on press corruption in the article *For Press Investigation*, published February 14, 1917.

Trilateral Commission, on David Rockefeller, http://trilateral.org/go.cfm?do=Page.View&pid=21 as of January 10, 2015.

Unterguggenberger, Michael, personal letter translated by G. Spiller, http://monetary-freedom.net/reinventingmoney/unterguggenberger-end_results_of_worgl_experiment.html as of May 31, 2016. Alleged original source: Annals of Collective Economy, Geneva, Switzerland, 1934.

US Congress, Legislation and stenographed discussion on the theme is archived in the Library of Congress, see for example House of Representatives, bill 240 from 1862, http://memory.loc.gov/cgi-bin/

ampage?collId=llhb&fileName=037/llhb037.db&recNum=1096 as of May 31, 2016.

The Koran, 2 Al-Baqarah, 275, http://www.noblequran.com/translation/ as of May 31, 2016.

Zaznobin, Vladimir, article in *New Europe — EU, Russia, Secure Future For Europe*, http://www.neurope.eu/article/eu-russia-secure-future-europe as of May 31, 2016.

OTHER BOOKS PUBLISHED BY ARKTOS

OTHER BOOKS PUBLISHED BY ARKTOS

OTHER BOOKS PUBLISHED BY ARKTOS

Lightning Source UK Ltd.
Milton Keynes UK
UKOW01f1050290317
297794UK00004B/171/P